OUT OF DOORS WITH HANDICAPPED PEOPLE

HUMAN HORIZONS SERIES

OUT OF DOORS WITH HANDICAPPED PEOPLE

by

Mike Cotton

A CONDOR BOOK
SOUVENIR PRESS (E & A) LTD

First published 1981 by
Souvenir Press (Educational & Academic) Ltd,
43 Great Russell Street, London WC1B 3PA
and simultaneously in Canada

ISBN 0 285 64934 5 (casebound)
ISBN 0 285 64935 3 (paperback)

Phototypeset by Servis Filmsetting Ltd, Manchester

Printed in Great Britain by
The Anchor Press Ltd, Tiptree

ACKNOWLEDGEMENTS

This book is based on the work of the Churchtown Farm Field Studies Centre in Cornwall, which is owned and maintained by The Spastics Society. I should like to thank all the staff of the Society who have given such support to the centre in the past six years, and especially to Richard Gray who worked with me and advised me in the formative years. All of the staff, past and present, of Churchtown Farm have contributed to the ideas and projects presented here, and it is also they who have provided the enthusiastic environment that was needed in order to begin writing. I should like to thank all of the handicapped visitors to the centre, who have regularly attended our courses and without whom no part of this book could ever have been written. I hope that they enjoy reading about themselves and their activities.

A very great contribution has been made by Sue Leake, who has produced most of the illustrations. She has been assisted by Jennie Hepworth, who illustrated chapter 2, and by Bev Woods (figs. 1.9; 4.17) and Peter Macfadyen (fig. 3.1). Other illustrations are by myself.

The photographs were taken by David Owens and myself, except for Photo 20 for which I thank Ronald G. Oulds (Billingshurst). To all members of the Churchtown team go my thanks. Much of the work has been shared with my wife, Sue, who has typed and checked the manuscript and given constant support while I was compiling and writing the book.

Finally, this book is dedicated to the memory of my friend Philip Varcoe, OBE, without whom Churchtown Farm would never have been. He provided our buildings and land, gave continued support as President of our 'Friends' and would have loved to have read this book.

CONTENTS

FOREWORD

It gives me real pleasure to write a foreword to this book. I have known Mike Cotton for a long time, ever since he was a young "up and coming" academic ecologist with a real flair both for teaching and research. He gave up a very promising career in higher education to run a field centre for handicapped people. The heads shook and tongues wagged in the halls of academia, I am ashamed to say that mine was amongst them, saying "what a waste of a good brain".

Mike worked at the Churchtown Farm Centre and the contents of this book have proved us all wrong.

Last year it was my honour to open a very special nature trail at a school for mentally handicapped spastic children in Sussex. As I journeyed down on the train the same doubts crossed my mind. How could disabled children, many confined to wheelchairs, ever manage on a nature trail, and could they really get anything out of such an experience? To add to my concern, it was pouring, and I mean pouring, with rain.

As soon as I got on the trail, all my doubts and worries disappeared.

The trail itself is made of concrete, a must to get the trail chariots (wheel chairs to the uninitiated) around. But the concrete was all knobbly to give a sense of soil, and it twisted and wound from vantage point to vantage point through a small wood. There were hides for watching birds – and one of these was connected by a wooden bridge to a platform built around a tree. Yes, everyone was able to climb a tree, such a simple and joyous thing which we able-bodied take for granted.

The highlight of the trail for all of us was the opening of the traps. I hasten to say that they were Longworth traps, designed not to harm their captives in any way. Without being there it is difficult to share to the full the delight of the gathered soaking throng as each child opened a trap, removed the warm, dry bedding, and discovered for her or himself what small mammals lived on their nature trail.

Thank you Mike Cotton for everything you have done, and everything this book will do to give so many other people these experiences and many more.

David Bellamy
April 1981

PREFACE

The out of doors has always been recognised as playing an important part in the development of children, even very young ones. 'Go outside and play' says the mother to her young child, and teachers say the same to their pupils in the primary school. 'Let's go outside then' say older children themselves. For most people the out of doors expands their own immediate environment – a room, the house, school or hospital; increasing the range of stimuli: 'Perhaps we will just go for a short walk' remains an urge of many who are elderly. It is important to create excitement in the minds of all people, and excitement can always be found in the outdoors scene.

For those who are in any way handicapped, whether physically or mentally, access to the outdoors and to the stimuli to be found there may in the nature of things be limited. Yet the out of doors should not be ignored; it is a resource that we must – and can – exploit to its maximum.

This book is designed for those who wish to expand their horizons. It is the readership, rather than the contents, which is new. Parents, teachers, therapists, recreation officers and anyone else concerned with those who are mentally or physically handicapped, will find it useful in their planning. So will young handicapped people themselves.

Equally it is true that many who are not concerned with handicap will find this book of value in presenting the environment to young people in Junior or Secondary schools. There has been a considerable expansion in environmental teaching over recent years, and the natural progression followed here could form a very suitable basis for an environmental studies curriculum. Thus, the urban environment moves logically from city centre to the parks and gardens of the outskirts, connection being made by looking at transport and the roadside verge. Hedgerows link parkland with more open countryside – first farms and woods, and as the journey away from the city proceeds we encounter rivers, lakes, moors and mountains.

Holidays, visits or walks, all bring us into new environments; but what shall we do when we get there? How do we get maximum advantage from a week at the coast, a visit to the castle or a walk through the park? In the following pages situations like these are described and topics suggested for investigation, both out of doors and on returning to home or school. Throughout the book we attempt to show how the 'outdoors can be brought indoors' by starting collections, keeping animals and plants, and doing simple experiments. Although essentially practical in nature, the project studies are set against a background of theory, enabling both the pupil and the instructor to understand more fully the environment in which they live.

Chapters are organised around different environments – the sea coast, farmland or the city – and each is briefly introduced by an account of the history of that environment within the British Isles. The establishment of woodlands, effects of the Ice Ages, and the impact of man are typical of these accounts. This is followed by a more detailed treatment of many aspects of that environment, indicating throughout project studies which can be undertaken by the pupil. Practical instructions are included for making your own equipment and using it, and we suggest a variety of ways in which the information gained can be used. Project studies are suitable either for group investigation as a class or for individuals at home, and there is ample scope for both in the material presented in this book. Clearly, not every investigation will be suitable for each handicapped person. Some will be especially suitable for mentally handicapped people, because of the immediacy of the topic, or because it involves physical skills which the physically handicapped do not have. Other long-term projects, or those necessitating a more demanding intellectual approach, will appeal to those with a physical handicap. In either case there is a great deal that can be done by anyone who is handicapped, and it is hoped that this book will encourage for all the pure enjoyment of life out of doors.

1 INTRODUCTION

Environmental education

Field studies and the handicapped
The Churchtown Farm Field Studies Centre

Collecting, observing and recording
  The camera
  The dark room

Project studies
  A church visit
  The weather
  Our river

Environmental education

During the past decade there has been a vast expansion of environmental education within schools and colleges, and environmental awareness among the public. We have become more conscious about the world in which we live, both in our immediate surroundings and on a global scale. A new language has developed: ecology, conservation, resources, pollution. . . . all words that we have grown accustomed to on television and in newspapers. We debate the energy crisis, population explosion and world resources; hard wood timber in the Amazon, oil in the Middle East, and pesticides in Antarctica – our environment has expanded world wide. With awareness we have found interest. Programmes about people and wildlife in far-away lands, and how man and nature interact, are popular television viewing and occupy peak times on our screens.

But, it must be asked, can environmental education be a subject in its own right? Is it not rather an approach to education as a whole? All too often 'Environmental studies' becomes simply a modern title for an old subject – nature studies, biology, geography or history. True, we have developed new courses at all levels from CSE, 'O' and 'A' level, to Honours degree, in Environmental Sciences and Human Ecology, but are these merely a series of integrated but inter-disciplinary courses? For an important educational advantage to be gained from environmental topics is the non-compartmental approach, as distinct from traditional subject-based learning.

For example, a study of traffic problems in your own town necessitates several types of learning approach. How much traffic is there? What constitutes the major problem? Where is it going? Does it cause significant air pollution? Is the noise level acceptable to people? Can we redesign the traffic system? Environmental studies allow us to identify a problem, research the situation and finally seek an answer, which is never simple and always involves a variety of wide-ranging opinions.

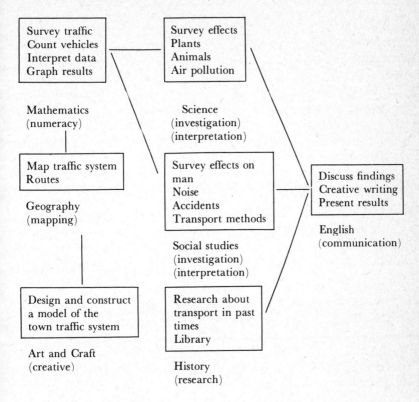

Fig. 1.1 A flow diagram of a typical Environmental Study on town traffic to demonstrate curriculum subjects involved and skills to be developed.

In most educational circumstances, environmental education will be considered as a *means of approach*, and it is in this context that we see the role of the environment in the education of the handicapped child. Traditional subjects gain greater significance and meaning when treated in an environmental context. Relevance to situations immediately meaningful to the child facilitates the learning process. There are few components of the curriculum that are not involved when we begin an environmental study, and in schools where such an approach has been introduced there is invariably greater stimulation and motivation of the children: 'I like environmental studies because we go out and discover new things'; 'I like it because getting out and about helps you to remember more about it'.

The child may be stimulated by creating an atmosphere within the home or classroom relevant to a particular environmental topic for study. Music can be used, for instance: there are compositions, both modern and classical, to evoke an atmosphere of the sea, of mountains, the city and many other environmental themes. Or we can use our imaginations to go back into historic times or forward into the future; to create changes in the weather and in the seasons.

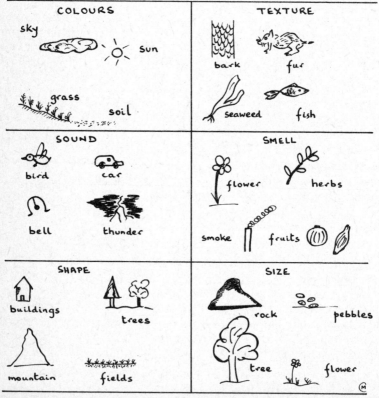

Fig. 1.2   Stimulating the senses – environmental conceptual learning

Certainly there are few skills which cannot be developed through the environmental approach. Numeracy, literacy, communication and creativity are all skills which we consider vital to expand in the early, formative years of a child's development. And some aspects of conceptual learning may well be best developed through an environmental approach – colours, for instance. This is especially significant for the slow-learning child and the mentally handicapped. Green grass, blue sky, brown earth and yellow sun are meaningful parts of the environment, which may well stimulate the child more, and promote better retention of information, than colours on wooden blocks or in a picture book. Shape, texture, smell, sound are all concepts that we seek to develop as early as possible in the mind of the young person, yet for those with severe learning problems may still be shaky in adulthood. The learning process is continuous in child, adolescent and adult, and learning through the environment has relevance at each successive stage.

Field studies and the handicapped

Field studies and adventure in a residential centre have only recently become available for the mentally handicapped and those severely physically handicapped. Though field studies centres exist in most counties in Britain, only one or two at the time of writing have some facilities for disabled students. At Preston Montford Field Centre, near Shrewsbury, buildings have been adapted to accept wheelchairs and a few courses are organised as suitable for disabled persons. However, these are certainly not fully representative of the courses available for everyone else. Courses in outdoor pursuits (sailing, canoeing, rock climbing) are also occasionally organised for disabled participants at the Sports Council Centre, in North Wales (Plas y Brenin).

During the 1970s two new centres have been established specifically for handicapped residents. In the Lake District the Calvert Trust has financed an establishment overlooking mar-vellous mountain and lake scenery. Equipped with a swimming pool, the centre provides courses over week-ends and entire weeks, in a good range of outdoor pursuits. Some activities involve nature trails and bird-watching. The centre is designed with wheelchairs in mind, although ramps outside are very steep and there are limitations in the buildings.

The Churchtown Farm Field Studies Centre

The first out-door centre to be designed and built specifically for use by handicapped people was Churchtown Farm Field Studies Centre, in the heart of Cornwall. This was established in 1974 by The Spastics Society, and it is on its work that the contents of this book is founded. The study centre was originally a series of old granite buildings comprising part of Churchtown Farm, and careful integration of old and new has produced an architecturally interesting building in the midst of the village of Lanlivery. The centre is in part a teaching establishment and in part a hotel, and its rooms and furnishings reflect this dual role. The original granite walls are retained in the common room and dining room. An old barn now forms the link between two new units and encloses the ramp system to lower and upper levels. One new unit includes bedroom accommodation for a maximum of fifty – visiting handicapped people and their accompanying staff – together with the residential centre staff. The other unit has a teaching library, a well equipped laboratory and the heated swimming pool, which is the main leisure feature. The entrance to the centre has a large display area for exhibition purposes and usually portrays the results of visitors' achievements during the week. There is in addition a photographic darkroom, art and craft room, pottery and lecture/recreation room. The buildings have been carefully designed for use by all types of handicapped person and the centre is well equipped for a wide range of activities.

Many access points were incorporated to enable the visitor to make full use of the outdoor environment; a number of doors lead outside at ground level, to spaces where a variety of aromatic and exotic plants create different kinds of atmosphere. There is also a raised flowerbed with conifers, heathers and a rock garden. All this helps to produce a relaxed atmosphere for the visitor. In order to encourage interest in the immediate environment, a bird garden was created close to the front entrance, with carefully chosen cover plants. This has attracted goldcrests and marsh tits, as well as the usual common garden birds, to feed near the centre windows. Bird boxes have also attracted tit-mice.

Slightly further afield than the immediate surroundings of the centre buildings, about fifty metres down a path suitable for wheelchairs, is a nature reserve. It is wet marshland, two acres in extent, with typical marsh plants. Snipe appear in the wet grassland, and there are abundant lichens and a variety of trees. A pond, bird hide and paths for wheelchairs were built, mainly by voluntary labour. The path has a hard-core granite base, with crushed and rolled in-fill to provide a reasonable surface. The pond was left with its little islands undisturbed, and the overall effect is one of considerable habitat and species diversity. Small areas have been built around the pond and stream to enable wheelchairs to get down into the water, and this feeling of intimacy between the individual and the environment is continued throughout the field work. In summer shoes and socks come off! The area settled down very quickly after digging and was soon colonised by vegetation. In some places this has now led to management problems: some of the more robust vegetation grows through the path, pond clearance and even grazing. A natural depression was left in the path and the opportunity taken to provide a change of surface, with a bridge over the 'pond overflow' and a small waterfall. This has also increased plant and animal diversity, and some additional planting of Royal fern and sundew has been done in the permanently wet area created. The reserve area has a nature trail and a well illustrated trail guide assists those on the courses to observe a great variety of wildlife. A bird-hide overlooks the reserve and a good selection of birds can be seen feeding, especially in winter months. In summer swallows and martins dip over the pond feeding on the profusion of local insect life. The hedgerows are constantly changing their flora and the entire effect is continually of interest. Everything is accessible to wheelchairs, the hides, the reserve and garden.

In addition the grounds provide a camping site, often the scene of an evening round the fire savouring the catch from the day spent sea-fishing. Nearby, an educational farm has been developed in a complex of timber buildings, which house a range of farm animals. Jersey cows, sheep and several breeds of pig are tame enough to be handled by young and old alike. Goats, a donkey, horses and a range of fowl complete the farm scene, and most visitors spend at least one of their days among these animals, learning about their care and habits.

The field studies programme is offered in most months of the

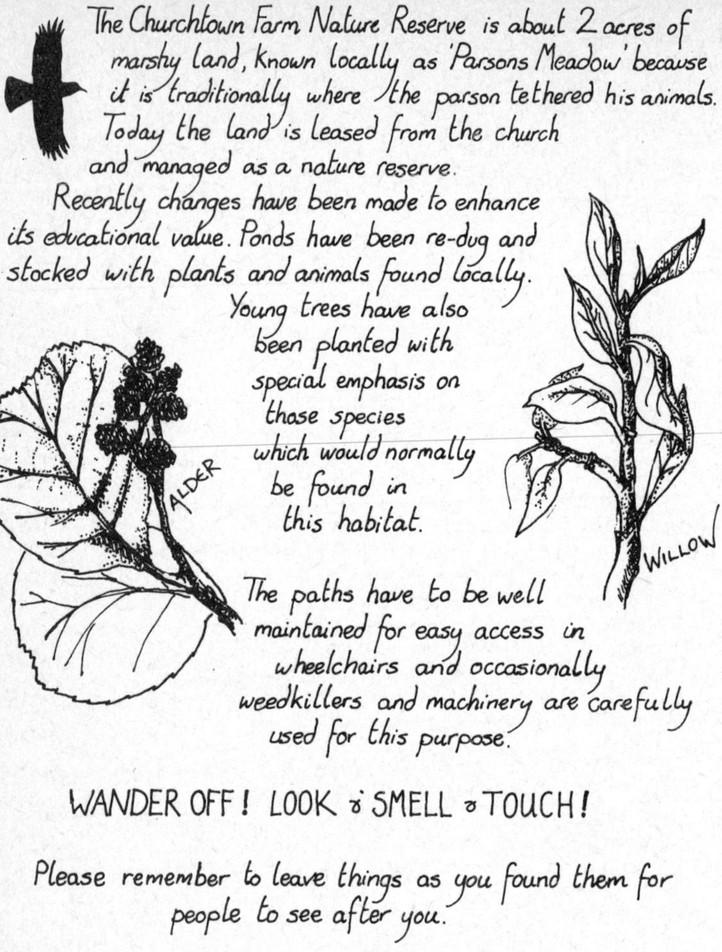

The Churchtown Farm Nature Reserve is about 2 acres of marshy land, known locally as 'Parsons Meadow' because it is traditionally where the parson tethered his animals. Today the land is leased from the church and managed as a nature reserve.

Recently changes have been made to enhance its educational value. Ponds have been re-dug and stocked with plants and animals found locally. Young trees have also been planted with special emphasis on those species which would normally be found in this habitat.

ALDER

WILLOW

The paths have to be well maintained for easy access in wheelchairs and occasionally weedkillers and machinery are carefully used for this purpose.

WANDER OFF! LOOK ♂ SMELL ♂ TOUCH!

Please remember to leave things as you found them for people to see after you.

Fig. 1.3 Design your own nature trail guide

year and can be arranged to suit the age and ability of any particular group. Young children or those with low ability follow a course 'Discovering the Countryside', involving daily field excursions to a variety of suitable habitats, followed by simple laboratory studies. Microscopic examination of living specimens is popular with all. And aquaria, of pond or seashore life, are fun to establish and observe: live animals are always

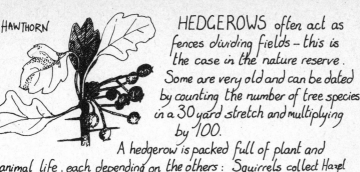

HAWTHORN

HEDGEROWS often act as fences dividing fields – this is the case in the nature reserve. Some are very old and can be dated by counting the number of tree species in a 30 yard stretch and multiplying by 100.

A hedgerow is packed full of plant and animal life, each depending on the others: Squirrels collect Hazel nuts and acorns and bury them for winter, some are never found and start to grow. Birds eat Holly, Hawthorn and Bryony berries which pass through the bird and germinate where they land.

There are other methods of seed dispersal: the Sycamore and Ash have seeds with 'helicopter blades' which blow them away in the wind.

A hedge contains not only trees which mostly produce masses of pollen from catkins for wind pollination, but also plants such as Primroses, and Foxgloves which have bright flowers to attract insects to pollinate them.

How many different mechanisms of pollination and seed dispersal can you find?

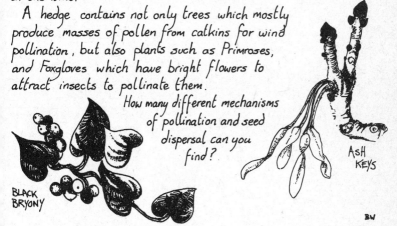

BLACK BRYONY

ASH KEYS

BW

better than dead museum specimens and ones obtained yourself are best of all! Equally, it is profoundly rewarding to observe birds from a hide in the morning, photograph them through a telephoto lens, and finally print and develop one's own pictures later that same day in the darkroom. More specialised courses include bird-watching, marine biology and various plant studies. Geographical studies on the Cornish landscape and on local history are especially popular, and most groups include excursions to local harbours and coastal towns, china clay works or tin mines, old castles or ancient monuments.

Adventure holidays at the centre include sailing, canoeing, riding, camping, climbing and trekking. Usually groups want to try a wide range of activities in their week's course, and they often combine these outdoor pursuits with field studies. A sea-fishing trip provides the excitement of a boat trip, the chance of a new interest in fishing and often the sight of seabirds and sometimes fish. Sailing has proved to be a good sport for both physically and mentally handicapped people, rock climbing has become very popular, and walks along coastal or moorland footpaths are guaranteed to produce plenty to interest the less able.

During the winter, the courses concentrate on leisure activities such as photography, painting and a range of crafts. Always these are linked with the local environment, and the groups undertake excursions to provide inspiration for art, subjects for photography, or raw materials – pebbles, rocks and slate – for craft work. Most people want to know something of the natural world around them; of trees, flowers, birds and butterflies, the life in a pond or rock-pool or the rocks and minerals of a seashore or moor. Handicapped people are no exception. It is the difficulties of access that often makes an excursion into the countryside a major problem: so the handicapped person at home or at school may lead a rather housebound life. But we have found that by adopting a positive approach, the wheelchair can be taken almost anywhere – across a sand-dune, or up a rocky tor, along a forest trail or close to the falling tide. Accidents will happen, of course, but one young girl was so enthusiastic about collecting specimens among the seaweeds that she overbalanced her chair and ended up head first in a rock-pool. In contrast to the horror of those around her, her only response to being soaked through was 'Gosh, that was FUN'. Many of the activities offered at the centre provide the kind of stimulation that is fun, and may also lead to a new interest for life.

The centre provides weeks for entire families, and a situation in which parent and child learn together; it is in such circumstances that the parent may discover a new and real ability in their child that is worth developing. Socially deprived children or those with behavioural problems also attend courses and in the new environment experience enjoyment linked with achievement. All groups are accompanied by a large number of able-bodied persons, often student volunteers who provide new social contacts and bring with them their own range of experience and interests.

Most of the techniques for working with handicapped young people that we have developed at Churchtown Farm can be adopted by teachers and parents for their own projects. This will become clear throughout the book. Before going on to develop teaching themes, however, let us look at some basic techniques fundamental to all project work; and then at a few examples of project studies which may serve as models for your own work.

Collecting, observing and recording

A great asset of the environmental approach is that it brings the child into direct contact with things. Children naturally enjoy collecting and this is to be encouraged and developed. We are not suggesting the child should pick every primrose within sight of the house, but that a bunch of wildflowers can teach a great deal.

Collections once made, however, need to be displayed and possibly preserved into a reference collection. Temporary display can be on a 'nature table', set aside at school or at home. This display should be constantly changing, with regular additions of new material contributed by the child at home. Labelling is important, and simple 'keys' to identify specimens may be found in books, or constructed by the collectors. Keys usually involve identifying just the more obvious features, which the specimens have in common with each other, then the distinguishing features, with final selection by features unique to that specimen. Thus, identifications are made by a process of elimination.

The leaves of six common trees, found on the way to school, can be used as a basis for key construction. In this key, the broad distinction between evergreen and deciduous leaves leads on to those between simple and compound, wavy and sawlike edges, small/pointed and broad/rounded, and so on.

1. Leaves shaped like needles, in groups of two, three or five –
   evergreen .... *Pine*
OR Leaves broad (turning brown in autumn) – deciduous   2
2. Leaves simple, each leaf arising direct from the main stem
   3
OR Leaves compound, each leaf consisting of several small
   leaflets 5
3. Leaf has a wavy edge, but not saw-like .... *Oak*
OR Leaf has a saw-like edge 4
4. Leaf small and has pointed tip .... *Birch*
OR Leaf larger, almost as broad as long; leaf indented where it
   joins the stalk .... *Hazel*
5. Leaf formed of 7–11 leaflets, each with a saw-like margin
   .... *Ash*
OR leaflets arranged like the fingers of a hand ....
   .... *Horse Chestnut*

Clearly, construction of a key to identification is an exercise in observation and not everyone will produce the same end product. Differences will be noticed by some and not by others, and each will consider some differences to be more important than others. The key arrives at an artificial system of classification, not based on evolutionary origins or relationships.

Observation of other specimens collected for the nature table may necessitate keeping the plants or animals alive for short periods. Flowers and twigs can be kept in water, and non-flowering plants such as mosses, lichens and fungi require humid conditions, best created in a clear-sided polythene or plastic box, complete with a lid. Many smaller animals can be observed in an aquarium or vivarium, which will need to be designed for the particular animals concerned. These can form part of the nature table and will be a constant source of attraction to the child. Remember that change is important – the display is designed to excite the imagination and produce interest, not to stagnate physically and mentally. The old jar of dying flowers, lump of rock and smelly tank of tadpoles will repel the child and do nothing for education!

Collections which are entirely 'home-based' and involve no 'outdoor' activity can still teach a great deal about the environment. This is particularly true of stamp collections, organised either geographically or on particular themes. Topics for thematic collections are numerous – insects, birds, mammals, wild flowers; crops, landscapes, industry, transport; climates, the poles, jungle, exotic peoples . . . stamp collecting is a must for all children at some time in their development, and will often remain a rewarding leisure activity into adulthood.

Recording techniques are usually based on writing and artistic skills – both areas in which a handicap may be particularly inhibiting. Physical limitations can make writing difficult or even impossible, although electric typewriters and electronic aids are often of great help; and lack of physical control may be very frustrating to the child when all his efforts to sketch or paint result in an end-product with little similarity to the original. Yet it is important to record what you see and notice in your project studies, to record changes and to describe the study visually. The role of photography here is greatly under-estimated. Few schools teach photography or use it. Yet the cost of photographic equipment, when compared, say, with the cost of a single electronic writing aid for one pupil, can be very modest indeed.

The camera

Children, are often first given a fully automatic camera such as the 'Instamatic' to use. This is not necessarily a wise choice. True, an instamatic is cheap to buy and simple to operate, but it has many limitations. Film must be purchased in packs, which you cannot bulk-load yourself, and the film size is too small to handle easily in a dark room. Colour slides (transparencies) too are small and not suitable for most projectors. So I would advise buying a second-hand 35 mm camera, such as can be found in photographic shops at no greater cost than the better instamatics. Such a camera usually allows you to adjust the shutter speed and lens aperture, to allow for differing degrees of light; and to alter the focus, to allow for varying distances between the camera and the subject. It is for instance very useful, if you want to photograph a moving subject, to be able to use a faster shutter speed (say 1/250th second) to freeze any movement and create a sharp picture.

Remember that a fast shutter speed will allow less light to enter the camera and it must be compensated for by opening the

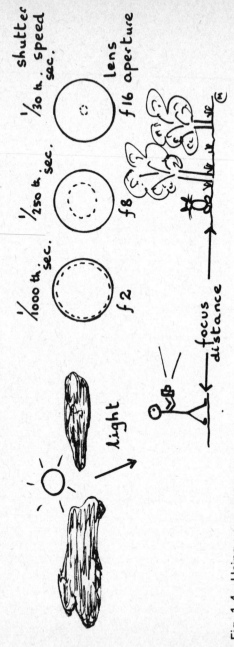

Fig. 1.4 Using your camera

size of the lens aperture. The amount of light passing through the lens to the film is therefore a balance of shutter speed and aperture. Black and white film usually has sufficient latitude of exposure to render any slight error by the photographer unimportant, but colour is more sensitive. And a fast shutter speed will be required by anyone who is unstable or has difficulty in holding the camera.

For those unable to hold the camera at all, it is possible to fix it on a tripod, or even to make a small adaptor to fix it direct to a wheelchair. The exposure can be made by using a bulb-release, purchased from a good camera shop (or even via advertisements in specialist newspapers). Here a large rubber bulb is squeezed with any part of the body (feet, mouth, hand), to make a change in the air pressure along a cable, which is attached to the shutter release button of the camera. In this manner a photograph can be taken by even the most severely handicapped person.

If you elect to use colour film, you will probably send away your results for processing, either as colour slides or as colour prints. There are many mail order firms which operate a cheap and reliable service, but you will do best to stay with one of the better known makes of film. This may be slightly more expensive, but you can become more selective in choosing your subjects for photographing: there is no need to take two poor pictures when one taken carefully would be sufficient!

If you decide to try your own processing, this will certainly be in black and white to begin with, although one day you may aspire to home colour processing.

The Dark Room

The school or home darkroom does not necessarily mean a specially built extension, although it is desirable to have a room you can darken easily, and, ideally, has running water. You can use a small bedroom, cupboard, the kitchen, garage or a classroom. First, design your system to darken the room. Blackout material can be bought for home darkrooms. No light should enter the room, since this will ruin photographic film and paper. Water can be supplied in a large clean washing-up bowl and jug. Work on an old table covered with a waterproof cover, such as plastic tablecloth, and cover the floor similarly with a sheet of polythene. Photographic chemicals do spoil clothes and materials.

What do you require?

1. Developing tank for processing the film;
2. An enlarger – buy an old secondhand model (e.g. Gnome) quite cheaply;
3. Three plastic photographic trays or dishes – to hold developer, wash and fixer;
4. Plastic measuring container;
5. A thermometer – to measure temperature of developer in tank and dish;
6. A safelight – to light the room when printing;
7. Photographic chemicals and paper – your only consumable materials.

Developing and Printing
The film must be taken from its cassette in *complete* darkness and wound on to the spiral of the developing tank. Skill in doing this comes with practice and the first few times will be difficult. Place all the things you need in front of you on the table, and practice locating them in the dark before you begin loading the tank. When you have completed this stage in the dark and the tank is firmly closed, you can return once again to the light. [Your cassette can be re-used by loading it with a length of film cut from a long spool. This too must be done in the dark but it is much cheaper to purchase your film in bulk.] The tank, with its exposed film, is now ready for processing, which takes about twelve minutes. Wash the film in the tank and drain. Add developer, which needs dilution according to the instructions on the bottle and making up to a precise temperature (about 20°C). The time for development depends on temperature and film speed, but is about 8–10 minutes. Agitate the film while it is in the tank and at the end of this stage pour away the fluid, wash by holding the tank under running water, and add a fixative (fixer). This is made up by diluting the concentrated fixer in advance. Fixing, with agitation, only takes a few minutes (2–5 mins), after which you may open the tank and examine the film. The negatives should have good contrast of black and white and after washing in slow-running water for 20–30 minutes, should

be hung up to dry on a clothes peg or clip in a dust free environment.

Printing the negatives involves a similar sequence of events, but the entire process takes place in the dark room with the red light produced by a safelight. The developer, wash and fixer occupy the three dishes or trays in that sequence. The temperature of the developer should be measured at regular intervals, as cooling will lengthen the time of development. Place the negative in the enlarger and compose your picture. Focus accurately and adjust the enlarger lens to an aperture of about f8. Place a sheet of photographic paper under the enlarger and switch on the enlarger lamp for a timed exposure. To begin with it is desirable to make a series of test exposures, of about 5, 10, 15 and 20 seconds each, exposing only a portion of the paper each time. Switch off the lamp at the end of this time and develop the test print for $1\frac{1}{2}$–2 minutes. Wash and fix in the respective dishes under the safelight only. When fixing is completed, one or two minutes, switch on the main lights and examine your test prints. The best exposure time should be noted; it may be between two of the actual times for which exposure was made (e.g. 5–10 secs). You can repeat the test, if desired, following the same proceedure, until you know the accurate exposure time for that negative. Provided all your negatives are of a similar density (relation of black to white), the exposure time can remain the same throughout.

If the negative is 'thin', too much light passes through and you must close the lens aperture and possibly shorten exposure time. Conversely if the negative is very dark or 'thick', open the aperture and extend the exposure time. Similarly, altering the position of the enlarger to produce a greater magnification of the negative will necessitate a change in exposure time, since less light is now falling on to the photographic paper.

Once you have made all of your prints they must be thoroughly washed and dried. Modern resin-coated paper requires no glazing to produce a good finish, and can be dried on a frame, or even by hanging from one corner in a dust-free environment.

Dark room processing can be done by very severely handicapped photographers, including those who must use their feet for manipulation. Usually photographic paper is held by plastic forceps in the dishes, but it is perfectly possible to place the trays on the floor and move the prints through each chemical stage of the process by means of the feet.

Project studies

While of late there has been talk of a return to formal learning, there is little doubt that project-based learning can be more enjoyable and thus stimulate the child more effectively. Projects have always formed a part of primary education and consequently are important in special education, much of which is based on primary methods. 'My home', 'Our school', 'The town' are frequently studied alongside traditional mathematics, english, art and history. But what of science? Science education is often neglected, reduced to 'nature studies' or at best, biology, or even ignored altogether, in primary and special education. This is a sad omission for modern man. Science is best introduced at an early age through the project system, where it can relate to other aspects of the study and not be treated in isolation. In this way, science as part of everyday life becomes a reality. Further, an experimental approach to other learning becomes possible with the incorporation of science teaching, which for instance often yields plenty of direct measurements for mathematical appraisal. Projects can be designed to occupy a short period of intensive study or to extend over several terms of the year. Some studies are worthy of investigation over even longer periods, though only short spurts of work may be involved at each stage.

1. A church visit – an example of a short-term project
Plan the project to involve as many aspects of the curriculum and as many skills as possible. Design your work sheets accordingly; allow ample time for follow-up work; encourage individual investigations, as well as group studies.

   a) Map the church and its surrounding buildings.
   b) How high is the church tower? What is the area occupied by the church and the churchyard?
   c) How old is the church? Into what historic period do its architecture and style fit? What has been the main historic developments since its construction?
   d) Make a sketch of the church. Design and build a model of

the church.

e) Write a short story about the saint after which the church was named.

f) Survey the tombstones in the churchyard. What is the oldest stone? Date 100 tombstones and make a block diagram to show the distribution of age of the tombstones.

g) Note the type of rock from which tombstones are made. Is this rock hard or soft? Where did this rock originate in the locality?

h) Collect the lichen growths on tombstones. How many different types (species) can you find? Are there more lichens on old tombstones? Are there larger growths on the older tombstones? Graph the age of tombstones against the size of lichen growths.

In this project we have involved many subject disciplines – geography, history, mathematics, language, art, science. We have also linked together many skills – map-making, measurement, design, research, observation and collection. Pupils can work together on certain parts of the project, do other parts as individuals and form small groups for model-making and tombstone studies.

2. The weather – an example of a project lasting a complete year
Weather makes a good topic for study at any educational level.

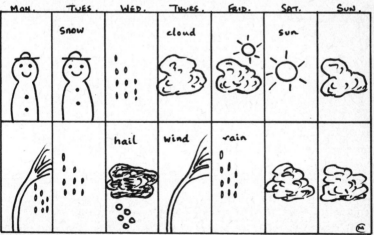

Fig. 1.5 My weather chart

Young children can observe and record, make a weather chart or diary. Older children can construct simple equipment, take measurements and record graphically. Weather is an ideal introduction to science teaching, enabling further study of pressure, atmosphere, temperature, water and energy. The weather is easy to relate to everyday life, to food production and to ways of living in other lands.

An investigation might involve a short period of measurement and recording each morning, followed by one afternoon each week spent in working on some special aspect of weather, either by research or by experiment.

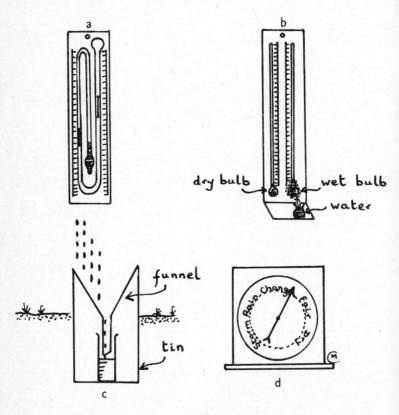

Fig. 1.6 Some instruments to record the weather: a. maximum and minimum thermometer   b. wet and dry bulb hygrometer   c. rain gauge   d. barometer

a) Construct items of equipment to measure temperature, humidity, rainfall and set them up in the grounds. Explain how each item works and how measurements are taken.
b) Measurements should be taken daily at the same time, and recorded.
c) Observe other aspects of weather – sunshine, cloud type and cover, wind speed and direction. Record.

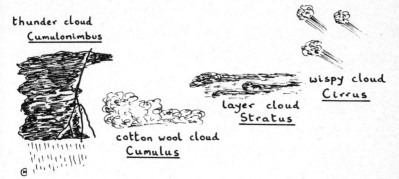

Fig. 1.7   Cloud types

Wind force

	Wind	Effect over land
0	Calm	Smoke rises vertically
1	Light air	Smoke drifts
2	Slight breeze	Leaves rustle; wind felt on face
3	Gentle breeze	Leaves move
4	Moderate breeze	Small branches move; dust and paper blow about
5	Fresh breeze	Small trees sway
6	Strong breeze	Large branches sway
7	High wind	Whole trees sway; hard to walk against wind
8	Gale	Twigs break off trees
9	Strong gale	Large branches blown down; chimneys and slates blown off
10	Whole gale	Trees uprooted; damage to buildings

Fig. 1.8   Wind strength (Beaufort Scale)

d) Construct a weather chart for the class, using symbols similar to those shown on television weather maps, designing your own symbols.

e) Each month analyse your results and calculate the number of days (percentage) for each major type of weather (dull, sunny, wet . . .). Construct a block graph for your monthly results. Plot daily changes in temperature and rainfall.

f) Make a study of weather in extreme climatic zones – a desert, tropical forest, high mountains, polar icecaps.

g) How does weather influence the way in which we dress; our houses; the food we eat; our life styles?

h) Learn more about the weather from the television reports – how can weather be predicted or forecast?

3. Our river – an example of a long-term project.

The long-term project might involve an entire school, with the older age groups undertaking the more difficult and intellectually demanding work, or it might involve one group of pupils throughout their entire period at the school. The topics of study will change with the age of the children, and it may be that the targets too will change over the period. In this example we are in fact looking at a whole series of studies within one project, each of which would be worthy of separate project status. One of the main advantages of such a long-term study is that we can witness for ourselves the natural and man-made changes in the environment.

a) Map (to scale) the entire river system and visit the river source and its estuary.

b) How does the landscape around the river change? Make a model of the river's course.

c) Find out about the history of the river – how was it used by man in the past?

d) Which industries are located along the river banks? Are they near the source or the estuary? Do they need water?

e) Collect and record animals and plants at each stage of the river system in each season. Does the natural history of the river change over one year?

f) Is the river polluted? What are the main sources of

pollution? Where does this pollution exert its main effect on the animals and plants? What are the changes in the wildlife?

g) Measure river pollution by both chemical and biological methods. Take samples of clean and polluted water and try to keep small animals (e.g. sticklebacks, insect larvae) in each. Use a 'pollution index' method to establish the degree of pollution.*

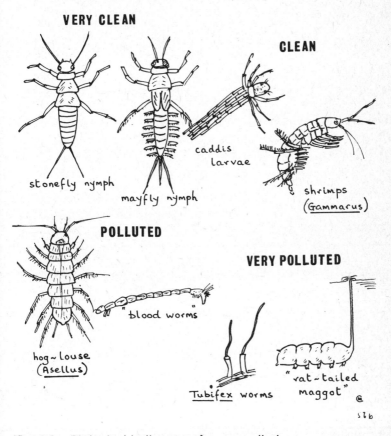

Fig. 1.9 Biological indicators of water pollution

* Water can be graded (1–10) from very clean (1) to very polluted (10) according to its' biological diversity and the presence or absence of certain indicator species. This is a 'pollution index'.

h) How is the river used for recreation purposes? Does the pollution influence these activities? Are attempts made to clean the river? Are there laws about the river?

In such a study we can monitor long-term effects, as in the extent and manner of river pollution, and allow for the educational development of the student. Thus, we begin with observation, mapping skills and historic research, and progress to an understanding of social factors, economics and law. The number of visits can be limited and the hours spent each year need not be extensive. Different staff can be involved where desirable to add their own particular skills, without interrupting the development of the theme. The project can thus take its rightful place in the total educational process.

Throughout this book a project approach has been used to produce an integrated series of studies covering many aspects of the curriculum. By linking many of them with adventure in the outdoor scene, we will provide the stimulating environment necessary for learning and enjoyment.

2 LIVING IN TOWNS

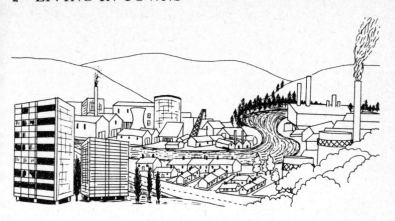

Introduction

The birth of the town

Town houses

Making a housing survey

Town trails

Shops and shopping

Town transport

Industry and work

Towns and land use

The zoo

City wildlife

Churches and churchyards

The roadside verge

Introduction

In this chapter we shall look first at how towns began, then at the wide variety of houses and buildings. A range of project studies follow, all of which can be completed in the town: design a town trail, investigate shops, traffic, amenities and industry, and then examine the city wildlife, both captive in zoos and parks and living free on wasteground and in churchyards. Finally, as we leave the city, we follow the roadside verge with its birds and mammals, and proceed towards open countryside.

Most people live together in towns and cities, and even those who live in the country require the services provided by the town. So most of us spend far more hours moving between one house and another, visiting shops and office buildings, crossing streets and negotiating traffic than we do walking in woodlands or on the seashore. Out of doors for most of us is the world of the town, and we should make the most of it, for towns are exciting places, constantly changing, and full of interest to the observant eye in the daily lives of people – their homes and transport, recreation and work.

The way towns are built profoundly affects the way we live. Some of us live in old and decaying parts, many more on vast housing estates; some live in the town centre, others at the edge in totally residential areas. If our house is in the centre we are close enough to the shops, our school and other services to walk there, but the further away we live the more important transport becomes to our living style. Buses or local rail systems must be provided. Many people have cars. In larger towns and cities, where more people live on the edge than in the centre, smaller satelite towns develop at the periphery, each with its own essential services, shops and schools. The growth of our towns has been greater in the past thirty years than ever before in our history but we must remember that all towns began as small communities, some of them in very early times.

The birth of the town

'Towns' it is often said, 'are as old as civilisations'. In the days before the invasion of Britain by other cultures, people in this country were nomadic, dwelling in caves or similar temporary shelters. Our earliest towns developed in the Iron Age, which lasted from about 700 B.C. until the Roman invasion in 43 A.D. Such communities developed as hill-top forts, protected by the rise of the land, by steep crags or other natural rock formations.

Fig. 2.1   Hut circles of the Bronze Age

Iron Age people erected defences and lived within them in earth pits roofed over with poles covered by twigs of heather or other local plants. You can find such settlements on Ordnance Survey (O.S.) maps, described as 'hut circles and hill forts'. When the Romans conquered Britain they developed some of these towns as military camps, and connected them with long, straight military roads (the Fosse Way, Watling Street), many of which survived to this day, forming the basis of our own transport system until the motorway era. Roman towns grew up throughout much of England and Wales, and in the border area from the Tyne to the Solway a great concentration of Roman settlements helped to keep this part of the Empire safe from marauding Scots. Most of these towns were fortified places, and the Roman word 'castrum' means a military encampment. Modern towns whose names end in a modified form of this word – Dorchester, Chichester and Winchester, Gloucester, Worcester and Lancaster – all began as Roman fort-towns.

The town was protected by a massive stone wall with a gate in the middle of each side. Much of this walled circuit can still be seen in some towns, such as Colchester, but in others such as Exeter only fragments remain. Every town was laid out on a grid-pattern of intersecting streets, with the centre or *forum* comprising the town hall, law courts, shopping centre and market place. Meetings would be held in the forum, which was the focus of activity and social structure. Roman town planning was fundamental to later development of the English town.

In subsequent years the farming Anglo-Saxons, who invaded during the fifth to seventh centuries, allowed the towns to fall into partial disuse, but the Scandinavian Vikings in the ninth century restored a significant role to them, especially in the north and east of the country. York, which was the capital of the Viking empire in that period, still retains much evidence of its Viking origins. The Roman walls of Chester, too, were rebuilt by Vikings, and the Scandinavian boroughs of Nottingham, Derby, Leicester, Lincoln and Stamford were established. The Anglo-Saxons regained much of their lost territory in the following two hundred years, only to be invaded by the Normans from France in 1066.

The borough of the Norman period was a defended stronghold surrounded by an earthbank, oval or square, in which the King established a garrison. The borough was also a trading centre with market place and an administration. Counties evolved, as land was allocated by the King to provide support for the defences and trading facilities of the borough. Thus Nottingham was a Viking borough, enlarged by the Normans, and supported by the territories comprising Nottinghamshire. The Normans concentrated their defence in castles, around which new towns grew up, seeking its protection and supplying its needs. Border towns such as Alnwick and cities such as Newcastle-upon-Tyne were born in this way, as Medieval castle towns. Much of the history of a town or city can still be read in its buildings today; castles and churches, defence walls and market squares. Excavations have exposed more of this history. The birth of any British town has an exciting story to unfold, told in its historic buildings and museums, as well as in books and maps and pictures.

Town Houses

Britain is a land of history and nowhere is this clearer than in its architecture. Our heritage of buildings attracts visitors from all parts of the world. Yet we, who can see them all the time, only too often pass them by without a second glance; upwards at roofs and frontages or directly at windows and doors. Period town houses are to be found in most of our older towns, or in each district of larger cities. Why not try to make a collection of your own photographs or postcards of town houses from different periods?

The characteristic 'black and white' houses of Tudor and Jacobean times had a black painted timber frame, filled in with a white plaster covering over interwoven split sticks. Inside beams were exposed in the ceilings, and upper work rooms were larger than the downstairs living areas or shop premises. The upper storey typically over-hung the lower row of shops. The woollen cloth industry at this time was booming, and new towns developed with the wealth produced. Money was spent by mill-owners on houses for their craftsmen. Today, such houses survive in several towns, notably in Stratford-upon-Avon, but perhaps your town has an inn or hotel of typical Tudor architecture as a reminder of Elizabethan days.

During subsequent historic periods town houses were built for comfort and elegance, and many towns, such as Cheltenham, Bath and Harrogate, became centres of culture and style in the eighteenth century. A craze developed among the aristocracy to 'take the waters' at spas, or natural mineral springs, and grand buildings, with pump rooms, were constructed for this purpose. In both buildings and furniture we recognise a change in style in the early eighteenth century during the reign of Queen Anne, and famous architects, first the great Sir Christopher Wren and later Sir John Nash and the brothers Adam, transformed English townscapes. During the latter part of the eighteenth century and into the next the wealth gained from the Empire enabled development of an 'Age of Elegance' in town building – the Regency Period. Small towns and large cities, have today

Fig. 2.2 Architectural styles of town house: a. Tudor   b. Regency   c. Victorian   d. Modern Revival

typical Regency styled terrace houses, each of uniform height and width, planned in intricate sequences of circuses, crescents and squares. Architects of this period were inspired by the classic builders of ancient Egypt, Greece and Rome, and they built immense columns to support porticoes for main doors.

Many towns of the north and midlands on the other hand owe their development to the need for labour for the Industrial Revolution. People flocked from the country to the towns where work and money were available, and large-scale building programmes produced a mass of 'back to back', undistinguished Victorian terrace and tenement houses, often in red brick, an endless repetition of deplorable living conditions! These houses became darkened by years of grime and chemical air pollution, the consequences of industrial growth. Coalmining, iron-smelting, textile industries all produced such industrial towns. Housing in Bath and Bradford, where the wealthy lived, was very different, and that difference is apparent even today.

The wealthy Victorian industrialists, mine and mill owners, constructed ostentatious residences and grand Civic buildings, bridges and railway stations. Gothic architectural styles, high vaulted roofs, spires and towers, rose windows, were all typical revivals in public buildings, part of the economic boom of the Victorian era.

Twentieth-century town planning saw a new development: with suburban life, the age of the commuter was born. Industry and commerce was centred in the town and city, while people lived on the margins, in a variety of properties according to social standing: 'mock Tudor' residences with gardens for the wealthy; detached and semi-detached villas for the professional and 'middle classes' and council houses for the working force. Later, as both population and land values increased, came the tendency to build 'upward' rather than 'outward'. Life in high-rise flats became a feature of post-war city expansion. Many

Fig. 2.3 'High rise' environment

families were rehoused, often against their real wishes, from slum city areas. Victorian developments were torn down to make way for concrete block buildings, offices, factories, flats and maisonettes. Towards the end of this century we are beginning to question our own housing development policies of the past thirty years. High-rise living has produced more problems than it has solved, and many such modern buildings now stand derelict and squalid from vandalism and neglect. We must think again about housing and city life.

Making a housing survey

A great deal can be learned by making a survey of houses and their distribution within your town. Obviously town size will determine how accurately you can map streets and houses, but in a large town you can make a small-scale map showing districts rather than actual streets. Initially you must classify or group your houses into a number of types, which will vary according to the historic background of your town. You may be able to categorise houses according to the historic period in which they were built; or the style of building and type – terrace, 'semi', or detached, flats, and housing estates. You will need a 'base map' of the town, showing streets and public buildings. A large scale O.S. map is ideal, but often estate agents provide town street plans which could be suitable. Place a large sheet of tracing paper over the base map and use a colour code system of felt pens to indicate each type of housing. Colour each block of houses or use a coloured line along the street for a particular house type. Plan your routes from home to school or the shops to cover adequately all parts of the town, making rough notes before completing that section of the map at home. You will be surprised how much you learn about where you live; about its history and the social culture of past generations.

Town Trails

Just as 'nature trails' and 'forest trails' have been developed in recent years in the countryside, so the 'town trail' has evolved to show points and buildings of interest and to tell something of the history of the town. Not all towns have well established trails with published illustrated leaflets, but you can make your own at home or at school. All of the information required can be obtained from the local public library or museum, and most towns have published histories. Once again the street map is essential. You will need to number each point on the trail. Begin at some well known central part of the town and organise the trail to form a logical route. In a large city it may be necessary to incorporate some public transport in the trail, to take account of long distances between interesting buildings and districts. The trail literature should give precise directions, and for each point on the trail a short historic account of the people who lived there or of the buildings, with dates where known. It should be well illustrated, with sketches or photographs. Many buildings will

Fig. 2.4 The town trail – some features to look for

have had a change of use and this should be shown. You may need to ask about the origin and history of some buildings from the current owners, although the Town Hall can usually supply this information too. Look especially at public buildings – cathedral and church; castle and guildhall; railway station;

town hall, museum and art gallery; schools and colleges; hotels, inns and markets. Modern shops and offices may be housed in old premises, which have been reconstructed. Look for plaques, monuments and statues telling of some famous resident.

The town trail can initially form a large display of material on the classroom wall ('Our town'); but you should also try to condense it into leaflet size, with street map, so that it can be used by others. Why not take the finished product along to the town hall, or perhaps to a large local company, and suggest they print copies for visitors (and residents) in the town?

The town trail is an excellent way to find out more about historic buildings. Visits should be made to all of these in your local area, even though access may not be entirely suitable for everyone. We have found that an excursion to a ruined castle excites the imagination of all. The able can scramble on to the ramparts and look down from on high to the surrounding land; but those physically restricted can still enjoy the sight of thick, stone walls, of old wells, and ruined fireplaces in rooms long since destroyed. Stories told or written can recreate the happenings of the past. Find out as much as possible about the place you are planning to visit beforehand, and try to use the atmosphere created by an historic environment.

Local Museums
The local museum is seldom used to the full by individuals or by schools, yet history taught in this way is far more meaningful than will ever be obtained from books or television. There will often be an Education Officer attached to the museum in a large town, who will also arrange visits with exhibits to your school.

Shops and shopping
Do you buy your groceries in the local general stores or in a large modern supermarket? Are shops of one type collected together in one part of the town centre? Which shops do you visit most often? How far do you have to travel to them? These are the type of questions we need to ask in a 'shopping survey', and we can learn much about the lives of residents from them.

We have always needed to trade, and in the Middle Ages the great trade guilds, of which a large city such as York had about sixty, built the guildhalls and almshouses and had a strong influence on local society. Market places permitted trading of all commodities in one place, and even today larger towns have permanent market houses or street markets. The modern town centre, with covered traffic-free shopping precinct, still retains many of the features of the market square, yet allowing for a larger population and greater comfort.

First you will need to make a plan of the town centre and shopping facilities. Perhaps you can do this in conjunction with your housing survey or town trail. Mark on the plan each type of shop, and grade each according to the essential nature of the things sold and how often you visit it. Thus a food shop or newsagent will be visited more often than a furniture store or shoe shop. Clearly department and chain stores and larger supermarkets will make a big difference to shopping patterns, since they sell such a wide range of goods. Try to assess the impact of a new supermarket on local traders. Are there many small, empty shops around your supermarket, where traders have had to close their business? The results of a shop survey can be presented either on a map or as a block graph (histogram), showing the number of shops in each category in your town.

Assess the shopping pattern of people of different age-groups, by producing a *short* questionnaire. Indicate yourself the age-group of the person answering and see whether the elderly have a different pattern from young citizens. Design your questions to tell what goods are bought in:-

1) Local shops – the village or suburbs
2) City centre shops
3) Supermarket
4) Shops in other places (larger towns or a city)

A visit to the shops can be a source of great excitement to a child, and many adults enjoy it too. Shops have an appeal; they are centres of activity and action, and attractive to the eye, especially where there are high standards of window display. Shops at night can be even more exciting, when it is late-night shopping in the city centre or even if shops are already closed. No child should miss the excitement of the city at night. Bright lights and bright colours are everywhere and shop windows take on a new appearance.

Distance from house may alone determine where we shop; but

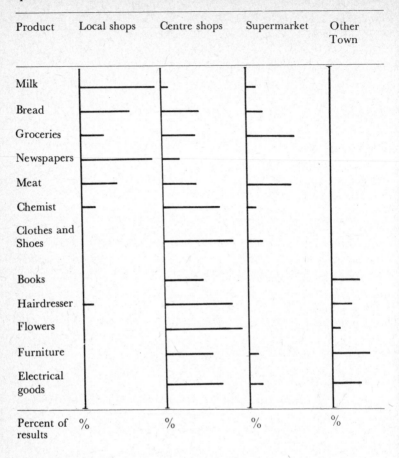

Fig. 2.5 A shopping survey in your town

our decision probably also depends on what other amenities there are in the local shopping area. You can carry out a local amenity survey and compare the results with those of other members of your class. First make a list of all services and shops you and your family use regularly. This might include a post-office, church, school and bus-stop; shops such as grocer, bread shop, butcher, chemist and newsagent; and other facilities such as a pub, fish and chip shop, or cinema. Now estimate how long it takes to walk to each place and make a total 'amenity rating' for the entire list. Mark on a map where each member of your class lives and the 'amenity rating' for his house. Do those who live further away from the town centre have a higher amenity rating? Are some districts of the town much better than others in 'amenity rating'? Are any facilities particularly lacking in your district?

Town transport

Transport, like other aspects of town life, has changed with the development and growth of the town. With suburban expansion public transport became essential, to convey the public to the centre for shopping and work. Some towns retained old transport systems, tramcars and trolleybuses, into quite recent times alongside more modern buses and local rail systems. An enormous number of people today use their own transport – cars, motorcycles or bicycles – to move from home to town; while on the other hand, as cities increase in size, and traffic and parking problems grow, there is a tendency to return to public transport. A variety of surveys can be made of local transport and traffic, involving counts by the roadside over specific time periods, or public questionnaires.

Design your own survey to take account of:
1) What forms of public transport are available in your town?
2) Which public transport systems are used for a) shopping b) work?
3) What is the density of traffic (vehicles per hour) at different periods of the day in key parts of the town?
4) What types of vehicles make up this traffic density a) private cars b) lorries c) public transport d) motor or pedal cycles?
5) Are the town roads heavily congested by traffic?
6) Is there a ring-road system to take town traffic away from the centre, and does it work? Is your town on a main route?
7) What is the car-park provision like in the town centre, for a) long-stay vehicles b) short-stay vehicles?
8) Does traffic in the town or on an adjacent by-pass or motorway create a disturbing amount of noise?

Some of these questions can be answered directly by counting samples of the traffic and presenting your findings graphically. A variety of techniques can be used to show the results – tables, block graphs, flow diagrams, maps.

Private cars	Lorries	Buses	Motor cycles
1 2 3 4 5 6 7 8 9 10 11 12 13	1 2 3 4 5 6 7 8 9	1 2 3 4	1 2 3 4 5

Fig. 2.6 The number of vehicles recorded in 5 minutes outside the school

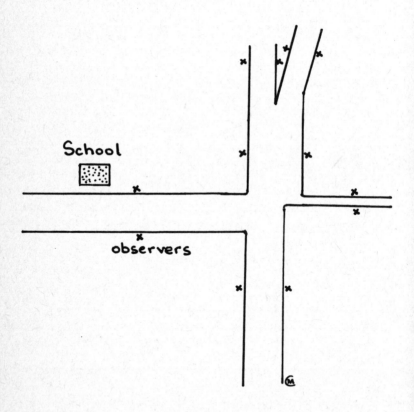

Fig. 2.7 A traffic flow map: the width of each road is equivalent to the number of vehicles passing each hour (1 mm = 10 vehicles)

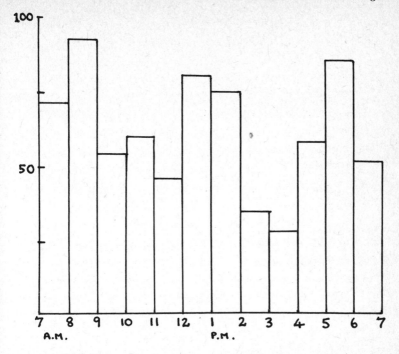

Fig. 2.8   Hourly counts of traffic flow outside the school

Industry and work

Most people live in towns rather than in the countryside because
this is where the work is available. Many towns have been
centred about one major industry which supplies work to most
of the local population. In some cases, the town may be named
after the owner of the company, who has provided housing and
amenities for the work force. Towns based on heavy industry
such as mining must develop where the mineral is found in the
gound – coal, iron-ore, china clay. Other towns have a wider
spectrum of light manufacturing industries, often providing a
service to other industries. Electrical and mechanical equipment, pumps and pipes, engines and transformers, and more
recently, computers are all needed by the larger heavy industries. Certain regions of the British Isles have become associated
with certain industries – coal and steel in South Wales, cars in
the Midlands, china clay in Cornwall and chemical industries in

Teeside and the Wirral. The location of certain industries is dependent on a number of factors, including availability of raw materials, power supply and cheap land to build on. A good water supply may be necessary for cooling and removing waste products, and often – in the past at least – for transporting essential materials and products, so many great industrial cities – Newcastle-upon-Tyne, Glasgow, London – are located on large rivers or estuaries, while inland cities – Birmingham, Manchester – are connected by canals to rivers. Water transport in the nineteenth century was cheap and efficient, and barges were once a familiar sight in central industrial areas. Industries also often have their own railway and even road system to avoid congestion problems.

You can undertake an industrial survey of your area, making a list of the major industrial companies in the town, using a telephone directory if you are unable to get out to find all of them. List the essential factors which must be satisfied for the location of each industry. Write to the public relations departments of the major companies, explain your interest and request they send you general information about their work and products. Many large companies and service industries provide well illustrated information packs.

Industrial visits can be arranged in the same manner, though this may be better done through schools or clubs than on an individual basis. Some industries have open-air working museums which show the techniques and processes of early days: at Ironbridge, near Telford, is a well-established industrial museum, and at St. Austell you can see how china clay was once extracted. Details of such industrial and local craft museums can be obtained from your regional Tourist Board.

Towns and land use

We have now made surveys of your town houses and public buildings, shops, amenities, industry and transport. Now let us look more closely at the whole picture. How often is it said that 'one town is just like another'? Is this true? Do towns have a common plan? In order to answer these questions we must make a survey of the town as a whole, and of the use of land in and around the town. Town transects are a useful tool for sampling changes in usage from the town centre outwards. A transect is a long, narrow strip across the town – you can select a straight route from a map before starting the survey. It is best to work as a group, each member recording details of one aspect of the transect – houses; shops; commerce (banks, solicitors, estate agents, insurance companies, building societies etc.); industry; amenities (recreation centres, pools, parks, gardens, playing fields); transport systems (roads, railways, canals, rivers).

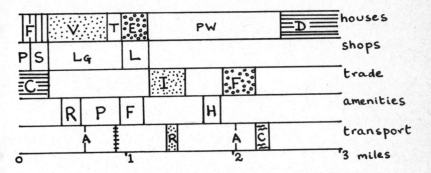

Fig. 2.9   A town transect: *houses* – F—flats; V–Victoria town houses; T—old terrace houses; E—council estate; PW—postwar housing; D—large detached houses; *shops* P—precinct; S—large stores and shops; LG—lower grade shops; L—local shops; *trade* – C—commercial; I—light industry; F—large chemical factory; *amenities* – R—recreation centre; P—park; F—football ground; H—hospital; *transport* – A—main road; R—ring road; C—canal

Depending on the size of the town and the distance to be covered, either begin at the town centre and follow your route to the edge of the town and 'green belt zone' (open countryside), or begin at one edge of the town and follow a straight line through the town centre and out again to the opposite edge. Record general changes and distances as you walk along, but list only broad changes in land use. Full details of the transect are best shown on a table, in a series of parallel columns, one for each component of the survey.

The Zoo

A major amenity in some large towns and cities is the zoological garden, and there is no greater attraction for children (and many adults) than a visit to the zoo. Such a visit may have to wait for the holidays, especially if it entails a long journey, but preparation for the visit can stimulate the child's interest well in advance, and enable him to enjoy it all the more. You can prepare by looking at pictures of different zoo animals, and looking up where they normally live on a world atlas. Small pin-flags can be made for each species, and these can then be fixed into a large traced map, spread on a piece of soft board or polystyrene or cork (a bath mat would be suitable). Colour the map according to major world climates and vegetation – desert, tropical forest, grasslands, polar ice, mountains. Which regions of the world have most species of zoo animals? Television features have brought many exotic regions of the world, together with their inhabitants, into the home of even the most sedentary person, and wildlife programmes are now among the top ratings. Children should be encouraged to watch such programmes, so that the zoo visit becomes a natural follow-up. Many zoos have an Education Officer, responsible for using the zoo as a teaching resource, who will be pleased to assist a group who are planning to visit the zoo, and may even take you round and talk about the various animals.

All too often, the zoo visit can deteriorate into a drag around the shop or cafeteria, because the children are bored for lack of interesting information about the exhibits – their lives, where they live, their natural food, adaptations and conservation problems. Find out as much as you can. Take along some good illustrated books and buy a copy of the guidebook. Follow the route plan and you will not miss any of the animals. Specialised 'houses' – the reptile house, aquarium, and nocturnal animal house – are all worth your time.

Some zoos have a particular interest in one range of species – the primates, large cats, bears – and build up a breeding programme for that group. The young animals reared in the zoo may replace older ones when they die or be sent to other zoos for exhibition, so that new animals need not be taken from the wild. In some cases rare species are deliberately captured, bred – usually in several zoos at once – and, sufficient stock reared, so young animals can be released again into their native habitat. Thus an endangered species may be saved from extinction.

These conservation measures have produced good results with the 'Ne-Ne' goose of Hawaii, which was reared by the Wildfowl Trust at Slimbridge. And in Jersey the famous zoo of Gerald Durrell is entirely designed to meet conservation needs; the familiar elephant, lion and tiger of most zoos are replaced there by rare species of bats, marmosets, reptiles and birds from distant regions of the world. This is a zoo at its very best. Though you may not have such an establishment close to your home town, there are now increasing numbers of wildlife or safari parks, bird gardens and Wildfowl Trust centres in many parts of the country where exotic species are a public attraction. Find out about them, and enter the world of far-away places.

City wildlife

While much of Britain has been submerged under houses, roads and factories, a great deal of wildlife has managed to survive in, and indeed exploit, our towns and cities. Man is not alone even in the heart of London. The pigeons strut in Trafalgar Square; massed starlings can be seen on their way to roost; housesparrows nest on the ledges of buildings; sometimes a kestrel hovers overhead. City birdlife is rich and varied. The London parks provide wildlife refuge in the midst of the buildings: over a hundred bird species are recorded from Regent's Park in a single year, and the lake at St. James' Park is always a scene of activity among the resident water birds. True town wildlife survives because of its ability to adapt and live close to man, and the most successful species are those which show the greatest adaptability: plant 'weeds' and animal 'pests'. For towns involve problems for animals and plants: problems of natural food availability, of lack of breeding sites, noise, atmospheric pollution and reduced light are but some of them. An organism that is rare, or disappears, is one which can be thought unsuccessful. City wildlife is a success in its own environment.

Dwellers of waste land – a classic example of adaptability and exploitation of new habitat was the colonisation of London bombsites in the years after 1946. Plant variety in the city increased from a few species to 269 different wildflowers, grasses and ferns by 1952. The city fauna also produced extraordinary variety by that year: four mammals, 31 birds, 56 insects and 30 other invertebrate animals. The black redstart, a bird once known only as a summer migrant, was observed breeding among the ruins, and it now nests in factory yards, railway sidings and power stations.

Although our city bombsites are now cleared and built upon, there still remain large areas of dereliction in the heart of any city. Rubbish and ruins form suitable nesting sites for many birds – a wren will use an old kettle, and blackbirds, thrushes or robins may build in the wreck of a car. Foxes can survive city life, dwelling on waste ground and roaming by night to gardens and dustbins, scavenging kitchen scraps. Rats and mice find a home amidst debris, moving between sewers, docks, industrial buildings and houses. In this way diseases have been spread in the past, and could still be today. Populations of 'wild' cats abound, and other escapees from the home such as tortoises, hamsters or guinea pigs may well survive on wasteland amidst a wealth of wildflowers. Rosebay willow herb, buddleia, white bindweed and ragwort are all common 'weeds' of waste ground, providing splashes of colour amidst red and grey buildings. Some of these plants have a story of their own. The Oxford Ragwort, which has yellow daisy-like flowers, grows naturally on the volcanic cinder slopes of Mount Etna in Sicily. It was introduced to England over two hundred years ago and planted in the Oxford Botanic Gardens. The seeds, dispersed by wind like the dandelion, thrived on the cinder banks of railway tracks and it was in this way that it spread to our towns and cities to survive on derelict ground. The leaves and stem of ragwort are the food plant of the black and yellow striped caterpillar of the cinnabar moth. The rosebay willow herb, with wind-blown downy seeds, is eaten by larvae of the elephant hawk moth, which, like the cinnabar moth caterpillars, is patterned to avoid predation by birds.

Flowers, mammals, birds and insects all exist in the city on wasteland. Why not carry out a survey in your own city? London or Liverpool, Birmingham or Manchester, all cities have extensive areas of derelict land where you can learn a great deal about plants and animals. List the plants growing there and find out about them. Where else do they grow? Watch for signs of mammals. Look in old bottles lying on the ground for remains of mice, voles and shrews. Look for birds nesting in the spring and summer and visiting at other seasons. What do they feed on?

Fig. 2.10   City wildlife – an urban nature reserve

Turn over stones and rubbish for insects and spiders, snails and other animals. Look at bushes for butterflies. Watch a local lamppost at night for moths attracted to light. The area can be yours and collections, notes and lists will grow rapidly. A long-term study over several years may demonstrate ecological changes, from early colonisation of ground through a series of development stages (or *succession*) to ultimate shrub and wood-land vegetation. With the stabilisation of a plant cover comes an ever-increasing variety of animal life, although with the arrival of each new occupant another may well disappear.

Similar processes are taking place, of course, in other city habitats. Railways, canals and rivers and their embankments

Fig. 2.11   Disused embankments – a railway nature trail

afford a refuge for numerous plants and animals. When railways are closed the line often becomes a nature trail, not always an official one. In the summer they are wild with flowers and shrubs – on one disused railway line I was able to show a group of handicapped children 146 different flowering plants, along a stretch of about a mile. Tadpoles, water boatmen and beetles were swimming in a large puddle, and eight different butterflies flew among the flowers. A grass-snake moved over the old line and a toad hopped into some gorse. We even found a site of the rare maidenhair fern in a cutting. A perfect introduction to the natural world, and an exciting walk!

It is surprising, too, what can be seen on a rubbish dump. Black-headed gulls swirl above town tips; herring gulls probe among the waste; carrion crows and other birds visit for a free meal. Many insects breed among rotting rubbish and provide food for other animals. A chirping noise in the evening indicates the presence of a cricket, and other relatives may include three different cockroaches. We produce an ever increasing amount of rubbish: a typical family of two adults and two children throw away each year enough rubbish to make a package measuring over six feet in each direction. In some towns, some of this waste may be used again or reclaimed as useful material – paper, metal, glass. Other waste is burned or incinerated in a huge furnace, and large non-burnable objects may be crushed prior to dumping. But even where such facilities exist a large amount of rubbish tipping continues, legally or illegally!

Churches and churchyards

An owl hoots; bats flit eerily between the trees; a fox creeps silently between the gravestones – the churchyard is awake at night. In a town, the church is often one of the oldest buildings and the churchyard may have seen little interference for over a hundred years. Mature trees afford breeding sites for insects, nesting sites for birds and cover for smaller species of plants. A well established churchyard is like a miniature wood in the midst of buildings. Old walls harbour beetles, woodlice, ants and other insects; cracks shelter a small fern; and the stone surface is covered by mosses and lichens. Ivy creeping over any suitable surface hides a secret insect world, or perhaps a lizard or slow-worm. The churchtower may be a suitable nesting place for swifts or swallows returning from Africa in the spring. Kestrels, jackdaws and barnowls too may nest in a tower, and pipistrelle or noctule bats roost or hibernate among the timbers of a church roof.

An interesting project is to examine the lichen growths of old tombstones. Lichens grow very slowly, and since the age of the stone is known from the writing on its face, it is possible to see how rapidly different lichens grow. Many lichens grow close to the surface, encrusting the stoneface (*crustaceous*), and looking like grey or yellow parts of the rock surface itself. Measure the width across the lichen growth and record the age of the tombstone. Repeat this for different lichen species and see if the

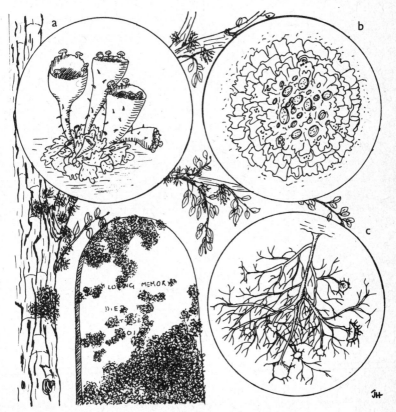

Fig. 2.12   Tombstone lichens: a. Leafy   b. Crustaceous   c. Foliose

older tombs have larger lichen growths. Do older stones have more species of lichen? You can plot your results on a graph, with the age of stones along the horizontal axis and the size of lichens on the vertical axis. Other lichens differ in their growth form; some are leafy growths, green or grey, often attached by 'root like hairs' to the surface of stone or bark; others are bushy or shrub-like growths attached at a single point to their substrate. Record a) crusty lichens b) leafy lichens c) shrubby lichens – in relation to the age of tombstones, where possible, or their presence/absence in the churchyard on walls, trees or on the church itself.

Lichens are highly susceptible to the waste gases produced when oil and coal are burned. Both the industrial and domestic use of oil as a fuel has increased in the past thirty years and, although towns have generally cleaner air than in the past, the level of sulphur dioxide gas in the air is still very high. Cities with problems of atmospheric pollution have fewer lichens than those which have had relatively clean air, and rural areas have more lichens than urban areas. Some species are more susceptible than others: shrubby lichens are very sensitive, and if you find them growing you can be certain that the air is clean of sulphur dioxide. Leafy lichens are more resistant, and crusty lichens can be positively tough and found in the most polluted towns. Lichens can thus be used as indicators of atmospheric pollution. The town can be divided into a number of 'lichen zones', from a central *desert* zone moving outward into cleaner air and open countryside. A simplified zone scale was used in the Advisory Centre for Education teaching pack on clean air. This contains a well illustrated identification chart, and some detailed notes on carrying out a local survey on air pollution. Lichen zones will depend on the direction of prevailing winds, especially in relation to some industrial developments, e.g. power stations.

The Roadside Verge
A journey by road can be an exciting venture, and a great deal may be seen along the many miles of our motorways and main roads. The roadside verge forms a 'linear nature reserve', affording protection to a great variety of wildlife. Undisturbed by man for much of the year, a dense grassland develops, interspersed at intervals by a thick cover of gorse, hawthorn and

Zone 0. Town Centre – no lichens but a green powder-like alga growth (*Pleurococcus*) on trees and fences.

Zone 1. Grey-green Crusty lichens (*Lecanora*) only on tree trunks.

Zone 2. Orange Crusty lichens (*Xanthoria*) on gravestones and concrete.

Zone 3. Grey leafy lichens (*Parmelia*) on trees and walls.

Zone 4. Shrubby lichens (*Evernia*; *Usnea*) on trees.

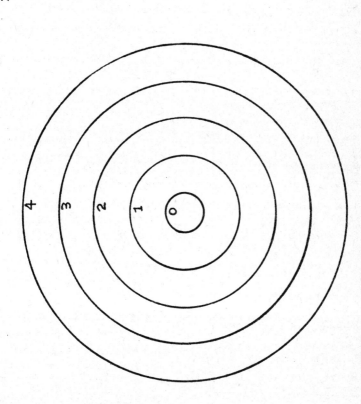

Fig. 2.13   City lichen zones

other shrubs. Trees may have been planted to give a landscaped appearance, or even to separate two lanes of traffic. This dense sward is soon home for high populations of the short-tailed field vole and other small mammals. The hovering kestrels seen along our motorways are anxiously awaiting sight of these voles, which are their main prey. In a recent survey conducted by members of the Young Ornithologists Club, it was shown that an average of two kestrels per mile were seen on the M6, compared with 1.5 on the M4, 1.3 on the M1 and 1.2 on the M5.

Fig. 2.14 The motorway scene a kestrel searches for its prey

The vibrations caused by heavy vehicles and other traffic cause earthworms and other soil fauna to come to the surface, where they can be pulled up by insectivorous birds or scavengers. So in another Y.O.C. survey members identified 56 different birds along motorways, a number unexpectedly. By far the most common were carrion crows and rooks, with starlings, housesparrows, kestrels, finches and gulls following in that order. Many animals are killed on main roads and their corpses become suitable carrion for such scavengers. Birds themselves are often involved in roadside accidents, and in a survey conducted by the British Trust for Ornithology over 5000 bird corpses were found on 341 miles of road. This suggests that over $2\frac{1}{2}$ million birds are killed on the roads each year. Many new roads cut through open countryside, farm and woodland, and mammals must frequently encounter a roadside boundary within their normal territory. Badger, rabbit, fox and other large mammals often cross main roads and motorways and are occasionally hit by passing vehicles. The natural reaction of a hedgehog to hearing a predator (or motor vehicle), on the other hand, is to curl into a tight ball, so that it is protected by a dense cover of sharp spines. While this might be effective against a dog, fox or owl, it is of little use against a fast-moving lorry or car, so dead hedgehogs or their remains are often seen by the sides of the road.

3 PARKS AND GARDENS

Introduction

Urban countryside

Conservation gardens

Garden life

Butterflies, moths and other insects

Birds and birdwatching

Birds in the garden

More bird projects

Seasons of the tree

A tree guide – what to look for and do

More tree projects

Hedges – history and management

Hedgerow wildlife

A hedgerow survey

3 PARKS AND GARDENS

Introduction

There is, as we have seen, a great deal of wildlife to be found in and around the town or city and the role of parks and gardens in sheltering urban wildlife is considerable. Further, while we may find it difficult to gain regular access to open countryside, most of us can find a local park and many of us have gardens of our own. Parks and gardens are urban countryside, so many of the topics we discuss in future chapters are just as relevant to town dwellers as to country ones. A pond, a river or a stream may all be found in towns; much parkland can be described as 'managed woodland'; and there are often hedgerows and heathland within easy reach of the city centre.

After a brief examination of the history surrounding much of our parkland, we shall describe how you can use your garden effectively to encourage and watch wildlife. We shall suggest birds and trees, and show how both can be studied through the whole year. Finally, we shall look at the hedge as an important reserve for plants and animals, and see how we can estimate its age and make a hedgerow survey.

Urban Countryside

Parkland has become 'the countryside of the town and city', although originally it was simply an area of enclosed grass and woodland used for hunting by royalty and the aristocracy. One of the earliest parks was Woodstock in Oxfordshire, which may date from the Saxon kings. Chillingham in Northumberland is another old park, enclosed in the mid-thirteenth century and now containing the famous herd of wild, white cattle, descendants of ancient forest oxen. Many of the famous London parks have similarly grand histories, and still serve as reminders that, London was once surrounded by primeval game forests rather than motorways and buildings. For instance, Richmond Park in

Surrey, with 2500 acres, was preserved by Henry VIII as a chase and still boasts fine herds of deer; while Hyde Park was taken over by that same monarch, from Westminster Abbey, in the early sixteenth century.

In later years parks began to mean the land laid out around country homes. This was the era of landscape gardening and of Capability Brown, who planned his parks as a compromise between natural wilderness and the formality of gardens. Woodstock was transformed with a magnificent lake, created by damming a local river, and formal gardens. In other parks vast quantities of soil were moved to create new contours. Even villages and churches were removed if they interfered with the view, and 'ruined' cottages were built to give the park a 'natural' look. The 'ha-ha' was a creation of this period. It was a concealed ditch that prevented livestock from roaming from their fields, yet did not interrupt the open view from the great house. In many historic houses and gardens, often today the property of the National Trust, you can see these features of the park era.

It was during the nineteenth century that recreation areas in towns and cities also became known as parks. Many were provided by local authorities under the 1848 Public Health Act as 'a means of exercise or amusement for the middle or humbler classes'. They still provide a service today for play, exercising the family dog, or simply 'taking a breath of fresh air'. Trees, flowers, birds and insects are all there in the city centre. Some parks create diverse landscapes with ponds and lakes, suitable environments for waterfowl as well as for model boat enthusiasts. Islands permit the birds to breed without being disturbed. Parks have usually good paths on flat routes, and many of the studies presented in this book can be undertaken by the handicapped person from a wheelchair in this part of the urban scene.

Gardens too provide an important reservoir for wildlife. It is estimated that there are $14\frac{1}{2}$ million British home gardens, amounting to a vast total area of 670,000 acres, almost three times the area of our National Nature Reserves. Access for the disabled to a National Park or Nature Reserve may be very limited, but most of us can get out into our garden. A garden is one of the richest of all places for variety of wildlife, and this applies to small town plots as well as to country cottage gardens. Much of this diversity depends on the gardener, and on his approach to growing things. Hedging plants, for example, provide privacy for the town dweller; but they also afford a home for birds and mammals. The gardener creates other habitats by building paths and walls, digging ponds and piling up the familiar rubbish heap at the bottom of the garden. Bonfires leave burned areas for recolonisation by small plants, and loose stones form a home for woodlice and black ground beetles. The garden pond is rapidly colonised by water boatmen, skaters and other pond insects, and even the undisturbed water butt harbours midge larvae and pupae. Weeds grow in cracks between paving stones and the uncontrolled lawn can become a carpet of daisies and dandelions. Yet, while in the countryside we call weeds 'wild flowers', make daisy chains to decorate a child's neck or collect dandelions for the 'home brew', in the garden wildflowers can become 'weeds', alien and undesirable species which need control by modern chemical sprays. Many are the food plants of caterpillars of colourful butterflies, which we then attempt to attract back by planting a buddleia bush. Common stinging nettles are eaten by larvae of the peacock, red admiral and small tortoiseshell – all common garden butterflies. Does the gardener always need to be in conflict with the natural wildlife of his garden? Are gardens and wildlife compatible? Can we create a garden which looks attractive and yet at the same time provides suitable habitats for our wild flowers, insects and larger animals?

Conservation gardens

Planning your garden with wildlife in mind can give great pleasure and at the same time assist animals and plants to live in towns and cities. Naturally it is easier if you have just moved house and the garden has been somewhat neglected, but a great deal can be done in the already established garden. First draw a map of your garden as it is now, with buildings, paths and walls or fences marked. Take measurements and draw it to scale, indicating the position of trees and shrubs which you intend to leave. Mark in the area of the lawn, crazy paving or other similar areas. Now we can begin to create diversity in habitats and plant life. First plant the more slow growing trees and

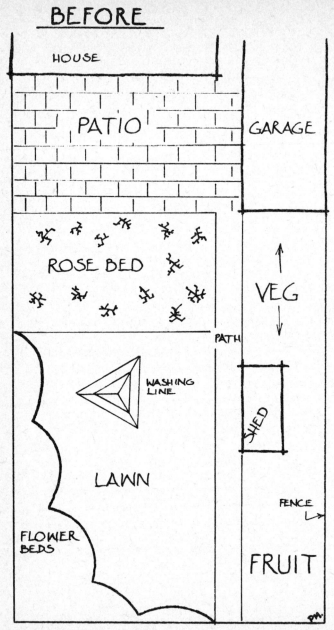

Fig. 3.1   Conservation gardening: how to encourage wildlife

AFTER

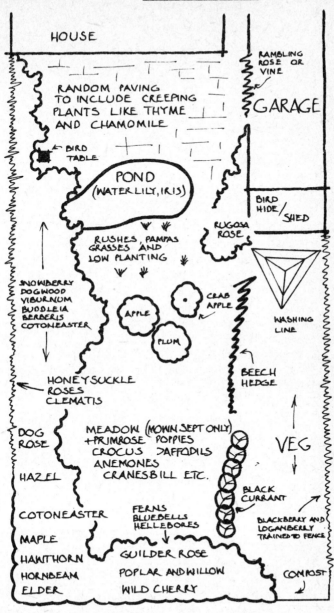

HOUSE

RAMBLING ROSE OR VINE

RANDOM PAVING TO INCLUDE CREEPING PLANTS LIKE THYME AND CHAMOMILE

GARAGE

← BIRD TABLE

POND (WATER LILY, IRIS)

BIRD HIDE/SHED

RUGOSA ROSE

RUSHES, PAMPAS GRASSES AND LOW PLANTING

SNOWBERRY DOGWOOD VIBURNUM BUDDLEIA BERBERIS COTONEASTER

APPLE

CRAB APPLE

PLUM

WASHING LINE

HONEYSUCKLE ROSES CLEMATIS

BEECH HEDGE

DOG ROSE

MEADOW (MOWN SEPT ONLY) +PRIMROSE POPPIES CROCUS DAFFODILS ANEMONES CRANESBILL ETC.

VEG

HAZEL

COTONEASTER

FERNS BLUEBELLS HELLEBORES

BLACK CURRANT

BLACKBERRY AND LOGANBERRY TRAINED TO FENCE

MAPLE

HAWTHORN

GUILDER ROSE

HORNBEAM

POPLAR AND WILLOW

COMPOST

ELDER

WILD CHERRY

shrubs which will take time to become established but ultimately will provide cover for many animals. Deciduous trees are
perhaps better than the faster-growing conifers, and we might
decide on flowering trees such as apple, cherry or almond. The
flowers in spring will attract insects, especially bees; the leaf
canopy will give a summer home to small birds which can feed
on insect visitors; and in autumn there will be fruit which can be
eaten by a variety of animals, as well as by yourself. Rotting fruit
fallen to the ground provides for blackbird and thrush, voles and
field mice and numerous beetles, moths and other insects.
Various shrubs and bushes can be introduced and grow rapidly.
The buddleia bush provides a mass of blue or lilac flowers every
summer, which smell like sweet honey and attract the larger
butterflies. The red admiral and painted lady migrate here from
North Africa, arriving in the spring, and small tortoiseshells,
peacocks and comma are all familiar in most urban gardens.
Bushes with winter berries are important to birds, the most usual
for planting being varieties of *Cotoneaster*. Some form quite large
bushes; others creep prostrate across the surface and are ideal as
ground cover. Rowan or Mountain Ash is a cheerful tree to
plant, with bright orange-red berries in October. Hedges can
have hawthorn or elder to provide winter feed, and of course
nesting sites in the spring.

In addition to trees and shrubs, a variety of other plants are
good for attracting wildlife. Thistles, some of which are
ornamental, produce rich supplies of seeds in autumn for birds
such as goldfinches; Michaelmas daisy, phlox, honesty and
aubretia all encourage butterflies and provide a colourful
garden through summer and autumn. Try, however, to let a
small part of the garden go wild. This could be along a hedge at
the back or in a far corner where the compost heap tends to
accumulate. Common wild flowers such as groundsel, dandelion, shepherds purse and nettles are all important to birds,
butterflies and other insects. This area can easily be screened off
from the rest of the garden by one or two shrubs.

Water is a must for the small or large garden. It adds
fascination for the child (and adult) of any age. Preformed pools
can be bought quite cheaply, but a hole in the ground, lined
with a double layer of heavy polythene, will make a suitable
pond. In a very small garden the pond can be proportionate in

size and only a few inches deep. Edge it with stones or build a rockery. Plants to the edge of the water give cover for birds who come to drink or bathe. Water plants can be grown in the pond and will encourage a variety of aquatic insects – beetles, boatmen, dragonflies and damsel-flies. Frogs and newts may visit naturally or be introduced to breed. You can collect tadpoles in jars from the local pond or canal.

For the child in a wheelchair, the garden should become the great out of doors, a place to escape from the confinement of walls, a whole new world. Hedgehogs and squirrels, lizards and frogs, peacocks and admirals, worms and woodlice, slugs and snails, birds galore, are all to be seen, observed, drawn and noted. Every part of the garden should be accessible and all senses should be stimulated. Herbs grow easily and provide a wealth of smells; bushes of lavender and rosemary, marjoram, mint and thyme, parsley and sage are all good for the stew-pot too. Smell them, taste them, rub them through your fingers. Plants of different appearance often have the same smells – like the lemon bush (*Lippia*), and lemon thyme, with its yellow-green prostrate stems. A small herb garden is a must for every house, creating constant interest and attracting plenty of bees and butterflies.

Most schools and residential homes have extensive grounds, which should create interest for handicapped children. Nature trails can be designed and constructed without too much difficulty. Paths are usually the biggest problem. In dry weather on well-drained soils a natural grass path may be suitable for wheelchair use, but in wet weather, or after much wear, this will rapidly turn into mud. So paths should if possible be built from hardcore, which is given a smoother surface with a suitable in-fill of small-size material. The whole is then rolled until it consolidates to provide a suitable surface. Timber strips prevent the hardcore becoming lost at the edges. In some localities the path could incorporate industrial or building waste to reduce costs. However, lack of permanent paths should not discourage you from using the grounds: it clearly makes no sense to society to provide access for disabled people to Nature Reserves and National Parks, if they are unable to go for a walk in their own school, centre or hospital grounds! Conservation areas can be set aside to encourage wildlife, and just as in the home garden a diversity of habitats can be provided by planting, clearing, creating water gardens or by changing the soil type in small areas. Thus, sandy soils can be introduced for dune or coastal plants; lime dug into the soil to create suitable conditions for chalkland plants, and peat-rich soils for moorland heathers. In this manner educational nature gardens can be established and common wild plants introduced from their appropriate environments.

Remember that wild plants are now protected by law, and you must consult your local police or Nature Conservancy office to find out which plants you can move from the wild into your conservation garden. The Society for Horticultural Therapy and Rural Training will give advice to any disabled person on gardening matters, or indeed anything else concerned with horticulture/agriculture. They produce a publication called *Growth Point* which contains a wealth of useful information, advice on aids, details on courses and meetings, and articles.

Garden life

Most small animals living in the garden are commonly regarded as pests and thought of as 'creepy-crawlies'. True, snails and slugs will eat your cabbages and dahlias, greenfly are a nuisance in the rose bed and ants frequently enter the house from their garden haunts. But earthworms burrow and improve the soil, honeybees, butterflies and moths are essential for pollination of many flowers, and ladybirds eat the greenfly from those same rose bushes. When we try to control the insects we don't particularly want, we must be careful not to remove the others which are beneficial. Besides . . . slugs and snails, greenfly and other bugs are fascinating to watch! A garden devoid of such animals would be a very dull place. Children love to observe the world of insects and their allies through the walls of a jam jar. Many different species can be found in the garden, representing a wide variety of animal groups.

Slugs and snails are *molluscs*, soft-bodied and often protected by a shell. They creep over the ground on a single muscular foot, at the front of which is the head and tentacles. Mucus helps the mollusc to glide along. You can see the muscular ripples if you observe the foot through glass. Slugs and snails rasp at leaves with a fine-toothed ribbon tongue, and this effective way of feeding is easy to see when they are captive. In winter, snails hibernate in sheltered places – under stones and litter, in cracks in walls, in the logpile or under flower pots in the garden shed. They make a tough seal of mucus over the entrance to the shell which protects them from enemies and from losing water from their soft body tissues. Snails are easily kept alive in a box containing damp soil and fed on leaves each day. Cover the box with a piece of netting, glass or wood.

You can make a vivarium for all sorts of garden animals. One of the most interesting to watch is the earthworm. Worms are *annelids* and have long bodies divided into numerous compartments or segments. The head and tail ends look very similar; the head is at the end which moves forward! Make a wormery by inserting two glass sides into two ends of grooved timber. The

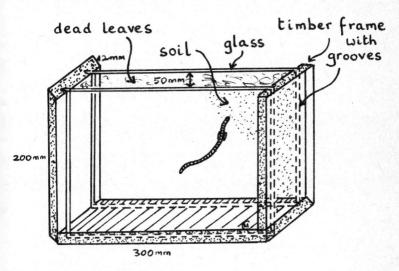

Fig. 3.2 Making a wormery

base is also wood, and the whole is filled with soil and kept damp. Earthworms dug from the garden or found in a compost heap can be watched as they burrow against the glass walls, dragging decaying leaves from the soil surface into the deeper soil levels. Worms are active under the soil by day, but at night they come to the surface, feed and mate. You can give them artificial night conditions by covering the wormery with a dark cloth. Observe when your worms surface – have they got a natural day and night 'clock'? There are many more garden soil animals which you can watch in a similar manner. Centipedes and millipedes are closely related to insects, but have many more than six legs. They are called *myriapods*. Their body is

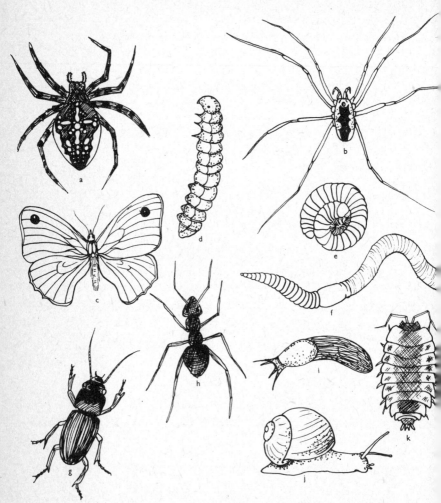

Fig. 3.3 Garden wildlife: a. spider b. harvestman c. butterfly d. caterpillar e. millipede f. earthworm g. ground beetle h. black ant i. slug j. snail k. woodlouse

divided into segments and they have a hard outer skeleton. But there the similarity ends. Centipedes are voracious carnivores, feeding on smaller insects with their pincer-like jaws, and millipedes feed on decaying leaves, rotting wood and other detritus.

Woodlice are *crustacea*, relatives of the seashore crabs and shrimps, and must live in damp, shady conditions, especially under rotting wood. They feed on decomposing matter and you can keep them easily in captivity, and do simple experiments on their behaviour in Choice chambers. These can be purchased from Biological Supply Firms, but you could design your own in a plastic tray, covering the whole with a piece of muslin or nylon gauze. Provide the animals with a 'choice' of environments (dry or wet; light or dark) and see which conditions are most attractive to them. Do the same experiments with other soil and litter animals.

Spiders and harvestmen have four pairs of legs and are *arachnids*. Their body consists of a large, round abdomen with a head which bears poison fangs and good eyes. They are carnivores, feeding on insects, which they often ensnare in a web. The prey, such as a housefly, becomes tangled in fine, silk-like threads. It is then paralysed by the spider, and all of its body juices are sucked out, leaving behind the dry husk of a body. Some garden spiders (wolf spiders) actually hunt for their food.

Harvestmen are not spiders. They have very long legs and small round bodies, which are not divided into two regions by a narrow waist like spiders' bodies. Their eyes are borne on a small turret on top of the animal. They do not spin webs but seek their prey of small flies and other insects at night.

Butterflies, moths and other insects

Observing butterflies is an ideal way to learn about the life cycle of insects. Eggs can easily be collected from cabbages growing in the garden, especially in late summer; but watch other plants such as nettles, too. Place the eggs on the leaf, in a screw-top glass jar and leave in the cool until the tiny caterpillars (larvae) hatch. They now need fresh plant food, the same kind as you found the eggs on. The jar should be covered in muslin to allow the larvae to breathe. Caterpillars moult their skins about four times while they grow, and you may need to move the larger stages into a bigger jar or a vivarium. A suitable container is made from a large sheet of *acetate* or clear celluloid, formed into a cylinder by sticking two edges together with sellotape. The base

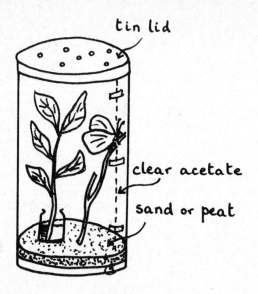

Fig. 3.4 Making an insect-breeding cage

of the hollow cylinder rests neatly inside a large tin lid and the top is covered with muslin. Place a layer of peat or good soil on the tin and a jar of water containing fresh food plant for the caterpillars. A twig provides a site for them to spin cocoons (pupate) and for the newly emerged adult butterflies to dry their wings. The adults can be kept in such a container for a while before release back into the garden. Pupation and development of the adult is slow, so do not be too anxious if you have to wait for several months for your butterfly.

Butterflies have feelers (*antennae*) with 'clubs' at the tip, while moths have fatter, hairy bodies and feathery antennae. At rest butterflies settle with their wings closed, but a moth keeps them open flat. Butterflies fly by day, feeding on nectar from flowers with a long sucking-tube coiled like a watch spring under the head. Moths generally fly at night, and often come inside rooms through an open window, attracted by light. They also fly to car headlights and to lamp-posts. You can collect moths by placing a lamp in the garden inside a clear plastic 'light trap' which can be made from clear sheet celluloid. However, if you stay with your lamp you can simply collect the moths as they land by the light and put them into a suitable container (e.g. plastic margarine cartons).

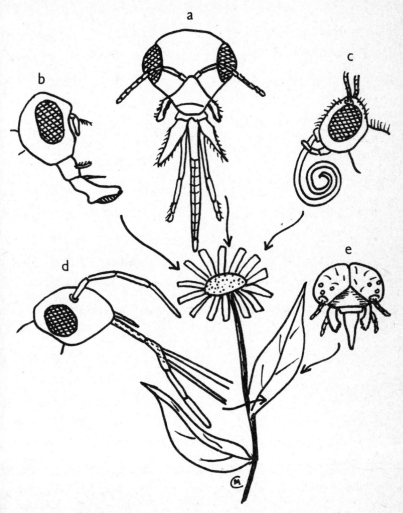

Fig. 3.5   Feeding and insects: a. honey bee   b. hover fly   c. butterfly   d. greenfly   e. caterpillar

The insect world is a large one, and you can learn a great deal from those you find in the garden. Look in every habitat – soil, dead leaves, under plants and stones, in wood, in cracks and crevices, on flowers and leaves – and record where you find each type of insect. Keep examples alive in a vivarium and observe their daily behaviour. Are they more active by day or at night? Watch them feed, since insects have a wide variety of mouth-parts adapted to feeding on particular foods. Watch their development – some young insects (nymphs) are very similar to their adult parents (e.g. grasshoppers, cockroaches, crickets, plant bugs), but others (larvae) are very different from the adults (e.g. butterflies, bees, ants, flies, beetles). Try to draw or sketch the young and adult of each insect you collect. Remember that you can see a great deal more with a good lens (× 10) or magnifying glass, especially when you watch insects feed.

Birds and birdwatching

Of all attractive animals there are none more popular than birds, and birdwatching has become an important leisure activity, indeed a 'way of life', for more and more people. For the handicapped person confined to a wheelchair, the bird world can provide special pleasure and satisfaction. One of the most important qualities required is patience. Wait, quiet and insignificant, by the side of the lake or river, shore or wood, park or kitchen window and birds will come to you. Often this produces far more success than a long hike over many miles or a noisy trample through the trees. Many enjoyable hours will be spent in winter, watching garden birds fly to and fro, feeding on scraps on a bird-table; or in springtime observing a pair of blue tits using a garden nest box.

Binoculars

You can, of course, see birds quite easily without the need of binoculars and many gain pleasure from their bird-life in this way. However, once you have watched birds through binoculars you will almost certainly want to have your own pair, and this brings us to the question of selection. First it is important that you can hold them comfortably for long periods – all binoculars become heavy as the day goes on. Buy a light pair, probably '8 × 30' or '8 × 40'. The former number is the magnification (× 8); the second represents tne field of view. Cheaper binoculars are often '10 × 50', which will be too heavy, and have too great a magnification for the field of view. Remember that it is *not* best to have the greatest magnification, since you will be unable to follow your bird easily in flight or to focus at short distance. There are several large firms which specialise in binoculars, cameras and other such equipment and you can find details of them in magazines such as *Birds*.

When you have your own binoculars, ensure that the strap is secure and safe and never knock them against a hard object, since this moves the prisms slightly and you will then see a double image. Dry them when you have been out in the rain and use a soft cloth or tissue for the lens. Keep the lens clean of dust and finger prints at all times – you will see far more! Adjust your binoculars to suit your own eyes:

1. The gap between the eyepieces should be the same as the distance between your eyes – not too close together or too wide apart.

2. One eyepiece, usually the right side, can be turned to focus independently of the other eyepiece. This allows for differences in vision between your two eyes. Look through the binoculars at some object; shut the right eye and look through the left eyepiece; focus the binoculars with the central focus ring.

3. Now open the right eye and shut the left eye; focus the right eyepiece, like a telescope, until the image is 'sharp'. Do not touch the central focus ring again.

4. Open both eyes and your binoculars will give perfect vision. Note the mark on the right eyepiece and this will be the same for your eyes whenever you use your binoculars.

5. Remember that a good pair of binoculars incorrectly focused or set is really of very little use.

The person with poor hand control or with neuro-motor handicaps may find that binoculars are too heavy and a monocular is more suitable. This can be purchased, but will not be half the price of binoculars, since monoculars are in less demand. They are very light and usually × 8 in magnification. If you are unable to hold your own binoculars or monocular, it is possible to fix them to a camera tripod. Few binoculars however are constructed with a suitable fitting, so it is worth asking about this when choosing your binoculars. But a handyman can make a suitable tripod-holding device using a camera fixing. Under other circumstances it may be necessary for a helper to hold the binoculars from behind and to focus on the bird, but while this is suitable for the stationary object it is difficult when the bird is flying.

Bird identification

There are many good books and field guides which will enable you to identify the birds seen. Some are arranged according to the habitats in which the birds live, others according to a more natural classification system of related species. Buy one to begin with which is not too complex, with good colour pictures, and which covers the more common range of birds. Identification comes with experience – look at the bird, note its appearance and immediately check with your book. In this way you will soon learn the more common garden and woodland species. But what do you look for?

1. *Size and shape* – relate the size to a bird you already know (wren, sparrow, blackbird, pigeon, crow, swan). Is it short and dumpy or sleek and thin?

2. *Colour pattern* – what are the obvious features? Colour of the head, body, upper and lower parts, wings, tail. Are there colour bars across the wings? Learn the names for each part of the birds' body (e.g. rump, nape) so you can describe the bird accurately.

3. *Beak and legs* – what shape and colour? Many birds have brightly coloured legs (redshank) and the shape of the beak is often adapted to the life style of the bird (oystercatcher).

4. *Flight pattern* – has the bird an undulating flight line or does it soar, hover or glide?

5. *Behaviour* – what is the bird doing? Does it bob up and down (dipper), wag its tail (pied wagtail), run at the edge of the sea (sanderling) or have any other obvious behavioural characteristics? How does it feed? Does it probe mud (waders), plunge dive in a pond or lake (ducks), peck at trees (treecreeper) or turn over stones and seaweeds on the rocky shore (turnstone)?

6. *Sex, age and season* – make sure that you notice that the male and female of some bird species differ quite significantly (the male blackbird is black with an orange beak; the female is a dull brown). Young immature birds often differ from their adult

parents (a young herring gull is mottled brown and white, the parent has fine grey upper wings and a pure white head and body). Birds in winter are often different from those in summer (the black-headed gull loses its black head in winter, retaining only a dark spot behind the eyes).

Bird recording
Careful notes should be kept of the birds seen on each field excursion, even if this is only a walk in the park or an hour in the garden. Your notebook should include details on where and when you saw each bird, and any particular features that enabled you to identify it. In this way you will learn your birds quickly and have a permanent record for reference.

Since many birds are more often heard than seen, sound recording can help a great deal in our identification. A battery operated portable taperecorder will give a perfectly adequate recording of bird song, especially if you are careful to keep background noise to a minimum. Make a collection of cassettes, perhaps arranged according to bird habitats (one for the coast, one for woods etc.). You can compare your own recordings with those on permanent records of bird song, which you can borrow from a public library. If you wait for the bird to appear, after recording its sounds or song, you will be able to name the species on the cassette. More successful recordings can be made using a parabolic reflector to concentrate the sound, though this is only really necessary if you are an enthusiast. People who must spend a great deal of time in a wheelchair, and people who are visually handicapped, often find sound recording an ideal recreational activity. You can bring home a permanent memory of natural sounds – bird song, running water, wind through the trees or the thunder of waves. I particularly remember the pleasure on the face of a young blind man, when he played back a recording made on a field excursion to the coast. The others could see their environment. He had heard it.

Birds in the garden
A simple way to attract more birds to your garden is by regular feeding, whether with kitchen scraps or packets of bird food. The former can be quite effective, especially if items such as chopped suet are included. Even the remains of the 'roast', or a

chicken carcass can provide good feeding for wild birds. Certainly nothing attracts tits so much as a 'nutbag', but this too can be made at home, with a nylon net, such as that in which oranges are sold. Fill it with peanuts, in their shells, and hang from a branch or the birdtable. Once you begin to feed garden birds, about November, this should be continued every day, since birds become accustomed to the regular supply. Once birds begin to nest in spring, feeding should cease, since nestlings often find domestic food too rich and require natural foods such as caterpillars. Leave a mixture of foods on your bird table – a piece of apple, orange or other fruit, some seeds, cereals, bacon rind, old bones with meat scraps, as well as scrap bread. Too much bread is not good for birds however, and it is best baked in the oven and then ground into crumbs. Try also to provide natural foods wherever possible, by planting shrubs rich in winter berries, leaving part of the garden wild and digging over an area of soil to provide earthworms and insects. Make a 'feeding chart' of different foods on your bird table and in the garden, and make a note of which foods are eaten by which species of bird.

Top Ten Garden Birds[1]		Nuts	Bread	Bacon	Fruit	Seeds
1	Starling	*	*	*	*	*
2	House Sparrow		*			*
3	Blackbird		*	*	*	
4	Chaffinch		*	*	*	*
5	Blue tit	*				
6	Robin		*	*		
7	Song Thrush		*			
8	Greenfinch					*
9	Great tit	*				
10	Dunnock		*	*		

Fig. 3.6   A feeding chart for garden birds

[1]results of a survey in January 1979 by members of the Y.O.C.

Your garden bird table is quite easy to build. Use a sheet of good board with an edge made from strips of dowel. The table size will vary according to your requirements, but should be

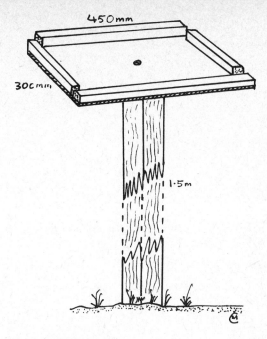

Fig. 3.7 Making a bird table

about 450 mm × 300 mm. Allow a gap at each corner for rain to drain away, and paint with a wood preservative. Screw the table to a wooden fence post set close to the house, where it can be observed from a window, preferably from sitting height. Your bird table is of no use if you can't see the birds feeding. But make sure that it is out of the way of the local cat – about five feet off the ground should be safe. A shallow area of water should be supplied close to the bird table, either in a dish or in a small pool which you dig out and line with polythene to make a bird bath. Keep the water free of ice in winter.

Nest boxes are easy to build, and if they are occupied by nesting birds will give hours of exciting birdwatching. Several designs are available, but basically there are two types – one with a hole at the front (for tits and other hole nesters) and one with the front half-open (for sparrows, robins and other species). Follow the pattern carefully and you can build your nest box in an evening. Nest boxes should be attached to a tree, wall or high

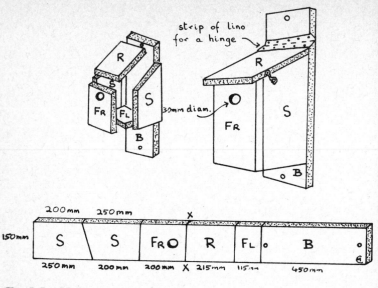

Fig. 3.8   Making a bird-nesting box

fence at about two metres above ground level. The entrance should not face the direct sun (south or west). Position it in late autumn or winter, giving enough time for birds to prospect for nesting sites. It is no good putting up your box in the spring and expecting nesting that season. Keep records of birds visiting each nest box, with dates. Note the type of nest material taken to the box (feathers, moss, straw) and the type of food taken for the young nestlings. Record the date when food is first taken and when nestlings leave the nest box. Do not disturb the birds once they have begun nesting, or when the eggs are laid, since this can cause the parents to desert their nest. It is also illegal to disturb or even photograph birds at the nest, and eggs must never be taken.

More bird projects
In addition to observing them, you can find other ways of enjoying them. Why not make a collection of feathers or wings from dead birds? You may find these by the side of a road, in a forest or at the seaside. Feathers can be mounted on white card or in an exercise book. Make two cuts (15 mm apart) and insert

the feather so that it is held in position. Stick the quill down with sellotape. Wings can be dried in an open position fixed down on a piece of soft wood with strong pins or nails. When dry the wing will remain open and can be mounted on card in a collection. Notice that the shape of wings vary according to the type of flight of the bird.

Bird skulls are also suitable for a collection but, need cleaning well first. Pull away most feathers and flesh with a pair of forceps and scissors. The remaining waste can be removed by a light boiling in water, but do not overdo this, or the skull will disintegrate. Finally it can be made white by placing in a dilute solution of bleaching liquid – but once again take care: bleaching solution harms your eyes and will also damage the skull if left soaking too long.

You can make casts of bird footprints using plaster of Paris, in the manner described later for mammals (see page 125), or you can investigate the diets of certain birds by dissecting out their food remains from pellets. Owls, particularly, cough up hard pellets of bones, fur and feathers – left-overs of the mice, voles and small birds on which they prey. Pellets can be collected at a feeding roost, beneath a tree, in an old farm building or by a church. Barn owls are especially suitable. Soak the pellets to soften them, and you will find that a great variety of skeletal matter can be separated out. Jaws, skulls, teeth, can all identify the prey species of that bird. Other birds, such as herons and crows, produce pellets, but it is not so easy to identify the remains within them.

Other bird projects are described in *Bird Life*, the magazine of the Young Ornithologist's Club (Y.O.C.). This is an excellent organisation and well worth joining, either as an independent member or in a group from your school or town. The magazine is well illustrated and gives information on identification, habitats, conservation, as well as quizzes, projects and details of birdwatching holidays. The parent body is the Royal Society for the Protection of Birds (R.S.P.B.), which publishes the magazine *Birds*. This is perfect for both the active field birdwatcher and for others who prefer to sit and just enjoy.

Seasons of the tree

Wherever we walk, in city or in country, at whatever season of the year, trees are a feature of the landscape. We plant trees in the garden, enjoy them in the park and even bring one into the house at Christmas. There is a strong bond between trees and man. Yet although it is not difficult to distinguish one from another throughout the year, many children do not appear to know the names of even the most common trees.

In summer the most obvious features of identification are the leaves; some simple (oak, elm), other compound, that is, formed of several *leaflets* (ash, horse chestnut). In autumn, we can collect fruits and seeds at the base of the tree and examine these. Then in winter the tree often appears dead; but it is resting, dormant until the following spring, preserving its stored food materials ready for a new bout of growth of wood and soft tissues. Even

Fig. 3.9   The tree in a) winter and b) summer

then it has a distinctive appearance – shape, twigs and bark – from which it can be identified. If you bring twigs indoors and put them in water, on the window ledge, the dormant buds will open early. The horse chestnut is especially suitable for such 'forcing' and as the sticky bud scales fall apart the lush, green, furry leaflets are revealed. Gradually they open until finally the full compound leaf appears.

When spring draws near some buds produce flowers, some of

which are bright and conspicuous but most are green, small and insignificant to the eye. Though tree flowers are seldom noticed, all trees produce them, and from female flowers the fruits and seeds will eventually form. The flowers of many trees are

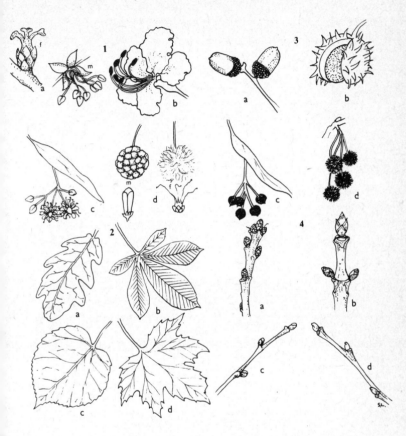

Fig. 3.10   Seasons of the tree: 1. Spring   2. Summer   3. Autumn   4. Winter. Woodland trees: a. Oak   b. Horse chestnut; Town trees: c. Lime   d. Plane; 1a male (m) and female (f) flowers from an oak catkin   1b. Single horsechestnut flower   1c. lime flowers attached to leafy bract   1d. female and male catkins and isolated flowers of plane; 2a, b, c, d. Leaves.   3a. Acorns of oak   3b. Horsechestnut fruit and seed   3c. Lime fruits on bract   3d. Plane fruits   4a, b, c, d. Twigs and buds

arranged in catkins, pendulous clusters of inconspicuous flowers hanging on a delicate stalk from the branch. The catkins may bear separate male and female flowers on the same tree (oak, plane), or as with poplars, yew, holly and willow, male or female catkins on separate trees. These catkins develop before the leaves appear, thus pollen borne by wind from the male catkin finds a female flower more easily. Petals are usually absent from catkin flowers.

Most trees are wind pollinated, but some, with bright flowers (cherry, crab apple, and horse chestnut), are pollinated by insects, attracted to the flower by colour and scent. Once the pollen from the male has reached the female flower, fertilisation takes place to begin to form a fruit, which will contain the seeds. The fruit is formed from the ripe ovary of the flower; the seeds from the ovules within the ovary.

In autumn the fruit becomes ripe and opens, releasing the

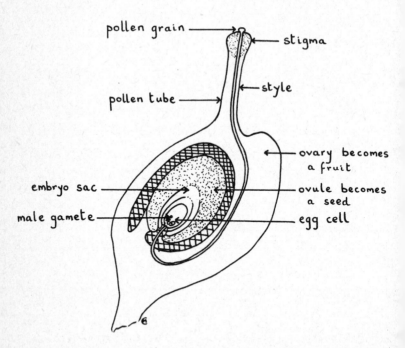

Fig. 3.11 How seeds are made: pollination and fertilisation of a plant

seeds, which germinate slowly when they reach suitable soil, to produce the new generation of trees.

A tree guide – what to look for and do

1. *Shape* – ask yourself, is the tree tall and slender (poplar), or short and broad (oak)? do the branches hang down (willow), are they gnarled and twisted (oak) or straight and fine (beech)? Practise sketching the tree to show different shapes. Does the shape vary when the tree grows under different conditions or in different places?

2. *Bark* – is the bark very rough, with deep ridges and cracks (oak) or very smooth (beech)? Does the bark peel away (birch) or flake off (plane, sycamore)? Is the bark covered in patches of sticky aromatic resin, resembling glue (firs)? Record the texture of the bark by making a rubbing on strong white paper fixed to the tree trunk with drawing pins or bluetack. Rub over the paper with a wax crayon and watch the pattern of the bark appear.

3. *Buds and twigs* – buds contain next year's shoots, leaves and flowers and the bud scales are protective. What shape are the buds – long and pointed (beech) or small and insignificant (elm)? Are the buds single (sycamore) or grouped together (oak)? What colour are they – black (ash), green (sycamore), brown (beech) or reddish (lime)? Are the budscales furry (magnolia), sticky (horse chestnut), whiskered (Turkey oak)? Do the buds alternate along the length of the twig (elm, lime) or are they opposite each other in pairs (sycamore)? Are there obvious leaf scars on the twig (ash, horse chestnut)? Is the twig covered in small, white spots or *lenticels*, which allow breathing through the bark (sweet chestnut)? Collect a twig and mount it on a piece of white card with strips of sellotape. Make a sketch of the twig alongside the specimen.

4. *Leaves* – are the leaves shed in autumn (*deciduous* trees) or is the tree green all the year (evergreen)? Evergreens may be broad-leaved (holly, laurel, rhododendron) or conifers (pine, spruce, fir). A few conifers are deciduous and lose their leaves in autumn (larch). Look at the leaf shape – is it a single leaf (simple) or is the leaf composed of several smaller leaflets (compound)? Examples of compound leaves are ash, horse chestnut, rowan. Has the leaf a smooth edge (sycamore), a saw-

edge (sweet chestnut) or a wavy edge (oak)? Has the leaf a number of definite 'points' (sycamore, maple, plane)? Are there prickles (holly)? Leaves of conifers may be long needles in pairs or threes (pines), needles in clusters (larch), short needles arranged along the stem (fir, spruce) or minute scales (cedar, cypress). Collect leaves from each tree and make a rubbing with pencil or wax crayon on paper. If you find a leaf skeleton under the tree make a rubbing of that too. Mount your leaves in a scrap book with strips of sellotape. Make an impression of the leaf in plasticine by pressing over it with a rolling pin; remove the leaf and into the mould pour some plaster of Paris. Retain the plaster while it dries with strips of cardboard. After about half an hour, remove the plaster cast from the plasticine and you will have made a permanent impression of the leaf. Collect leaves in autumn to show the range of colours for each tree (brown, red, orange, yellow). Mount these leaves in your collection.

5. *Flowers* – when does the tree flower? If there are catkins in winter or early spring, before the leaves appear, the tree is probably a willow, poplar, hazel, elm or alder. Most trees flower between the time of leafing (spring) and mid-summer (apple, horse chestnut). Do the flowers bear petals (horse chestnut) – how many and what colour? How many stamens are there in each flower – numerous (rowan), eight (sycamore), six (horse chestnut), five (elder), four (holly) or two (ash)? Does the tree have catkins? Are male and female catkins on separate trees (willow, poplar) or the same tree (hazel, oak)? What shape are the catkins? Collect male catkins from willow or hazel in early spring and put the twigs in water in the house. Watch the yellow pollen ripen and cover the catkin. Blow over the ripe catkin and see how light the pollen grains are.

6. *Fruit and seeds* – are the fruits soft and fleshy with many seeds (apple, pear), or a single large seed or 'stone' (plum, cherry)? Are the fruits brightly coloured berries, with four seeds (holly), two seeds (rowan) or one seed (elder, hawthorn)? Many trees produce nuts – hard dry seeds within a dry fruit or 'case'. The acorn is the nut of the oak, partly enclosed in a cup; beech masts contain several nuts; the horse chestnut 'conker' is a single nut enclosed in a spine-covered green fruit. Does the fruit have a wing to help its dispersal by wind, away from the parent tree? There may be a single wing (ash) or a double-wing (sycamore).

The fruit may be similarly flattened (elm), or borne on a flattened leaf-like bract (lime). The fruit may be a tight, round ball enclosing numerous small hairy seeds (plane) or, as in the alder, a small, brown cone. The seeds of conifers are naked with a papery scale and enclosed in a dry, woody cone: the cone can stay on the tree for years after the seeds have been dispersed by the wind.

Fig. 3.12 Autumn fruits and seeds: a. beech nuts   b. rose hips   c. hazel nuts   d. Old man's beard   e. elder berries   f. sloe fruits   g. blackberries   h. honeysuckle berries   i. horsechestnut conkers   j. hawthorn berries   k. oak acorns   l. holly berries and single seed   m. sweet chestnut case and seed   n. black bryony berries

Make a collection of fruits and seeds – they are easily stored dry, mounted on card or in boxes. Try to grow some young trees by germinating seeds. Acorns, chestnuts and sycamore 'wings' are very suitable. Soak the seeds overnight and plant in a flower pot in good loam soil or garden compost. (Provide some drainage at the bottom of the pot with small stones before filling with soil.) Place the pot in a saucer of water and enclose the top with a polythene bag, tied in position, to keep in the moisture. Place in a warm sunny window ledge and when the seedling emerges remove the polythene bag. Water – but not too much! Harden it off in summer by placing the pot in the garden, then plant out into the open ground in autumn. Try to grow seedlings by keeping them under various conditions – in the dark; in the cold; without water. What do you notice? What conditions do seeds need for successful germination?

More projects with trees

1. *How old is the tree?* The tree supports itself by producing wood inside the bark of the trunk and branches. The wood made in the spring is pale and has wide tubes to carry sap, while summer wood is darker and stronger. Each pair of layers forms an *annual*

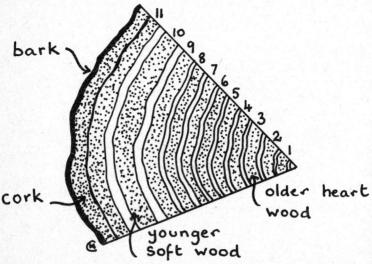

Fig. 3.13 A section across a piece of wood showing annual growth rings

ring and the age of the tree can be estimated by counting these rings (it is simplest to count only the dark rings). Practise on some sawn logs and tree stumps in the local park or wood. At the same time measure the circumference (*girth*) of the tree with a tape measure or length of string. Do older trees have a greater girth?

2. *How tall is the tree?* There are several ways to estimate the height of trees, which do not involve climbing them. a) Ask someone to stand at the foot of the tree. Stand well away from the tree yourself. Hold a pencil or stick vertically at arms' length with the top of the pencil in line with the persons' head. Move

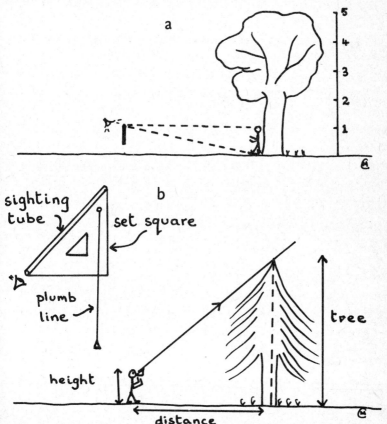

Fig. 3.14   Measuring the height of a tree a) sighting method b) the angle method

your thumb up the pencil until it is in line with the persons' feet. Keep the thumb in position and see how many times the part of the pencil above your thumb goes into the height of the tree, by raising your arm and sighting along the top of the pencil. This number (for this tree 5) multiplied by the height of the person at the tree base equals the tree height. It is most accurate if you stand at a distance roughly equal to the height of the tree.

b) Attach a drinking straw (the 'sighting tube') with sellotape along the sloping side of a set square. Attach a weighted piece of string (the 'plumb line') to the front edge. Hold this apparatus in position to your eye looking along the length of the straw (like a telescope). Walk away from the tree until the treetop can be seen through the straw, keeping the plumb line vertical. The distance from the observer to the tree *plus* the height of the observer (from eye to feet) is the height of the tree.

3. *Making a tree map* Take a walk from your house (or school) towards a local park, area of waste ground or small wood.

Make a sketch map of the roads, main buildings and open ground. Record the position of each tree on your map, listing the name of each tree. Are the trees along the roads the same as those in the park or wood?

Measure the height of each tree and estimate which species of trees are taller than others. Make a sketch of each type of tree.

Keep a collection of leaves, twigs, fruits and seeds. Take leaf and bark rubbings.

Follow the trees on your map through each season, noting when each flowers, produces leaves, fruits and when leaf-fall occurs.

Your local tree survey can add interest to a walk which you may take every day. It will also help you to know your trees! The Council for the Protection of Rural England will send you a free copy of their leaflet *Making a tree survey*.

Hedges – history and management

Hedgerows are a highly distinctive feature of the British landscape. They have been with us for several hundred years, mostly since the 'Enclosure' era when parliament determined that land should have well defined boundaries or hedges. Before this period of legislation in the eighteenth and nineteenth centuries, land was generally not enclosed, but earlier boundaries can be traced from historical records. County boundaries are among the earliest (ninth century), Parish boundaries may date from the seventh to twelfth centuries, and such important documents, such as the Doomsday Book (1086), allow identification of important home farm boundaries nearly a thousand years ago. Monasteries, large private estates, and medieval parkland all played a role in establishing boundary hedgerows, and some can still be found today. Traditionally hedges were maintained by layering (a process of weaving the branches together to form a strong barrier) every seven years or by coppicing (cutting down and replanting) every 12–15 years. Trees, notably hazel, which could be managed in this way were planted. The timber removed at coppicing provided hurdles, rafters, thatching timbers or firewood. The land was then ploughed and planted with cereal or root crops until the hedge grew up again, when the land could once more become pasture for grazing animals. Hedge trees, such as hawthorn and blackthorn, provide good thick growth preventing farm stock from wandering. The hedge provided a refuge for wildlife, prevented erosion of the land by wind and rain and gave winter protection to livestock.

Modern farm management techniques, using tractors to plough fields in place of horses, have made large fields easier to handle than small ones, so millions of hedgerows have been uprooted in the past 20 years. Chemical herbicides have been sprayed to control growth, especially on roadside hedgerows, thus affecting wild flowers and subsequently the insects, birds and mammals dwelling among the plantlife. Flail mowers attached to a tractor can crop a hedge more rapidly than an old hedger could layer or coppice it, but the appearance of the hedge is radically different. The torn, frayed branches of the recently flailed hedge are an eyesore for months, while the newly layered hedge was a feature to admire. Layering took place out of the nesting season of hedgerow birds; but the flail mower shows little respect for wildlife and creates a disturbance. The mower also makes no discrimination in favour of interesting hedge species – all go the same way.

A well managed hedge has a great wealth of wildlife, and hedgerows form Britains' largest nature reserve. In the early 1960s it was estimated that our hedgerow heritage amounted to half a million acres – twice that of our nature reserves. Since then some 5,000 miles of hedges have been lost annually, largely due to changes in farming techniques, but also due to road improvements and other building work. Hedge removal has enabled farmers to provide larger fields, giving more extensive acreage for cultivation and cropping of cereals by combine harvesters. This is especially true in the eastern counties where hedgerows can now be miles apart, thus isolating the remaining wildlife and allowing physical erosion of the land. In this way 'dust bowl' situations are created and soil is blown away from the land.

Hedgerow wildlife

Hedgerows are 'linear woodland', and as in all woods trees predominate there. Most species of tree can be found somewhere in a hedge. The richest hedges are those on chalk soils, where flowering shrubs like privet, cherry, yew and whitebeam are common. Oak, ash, holly, beech are all typical large trees of the hedge in the south-west and central England, while types of elm vary according to the region – the English elm in the south and midlands; Wych elm in the north and west; the small-leaved elm in East Anglia; and the Cornish elm in that county. Hedgerow flowers, birds and mammals are mainly typical of large stands of woodland and forests, although some birds are certainly more associated with hedges than with woods. Recent surveys by the British Trust for Ornithology show the most common hedge birds as song thrush, yellow hammer, chaffinch, dunnock, whitethroat, skylark, blackbird and robin. The skylark actually breeds in fields adjoining the hedgerow, but the others are hedge nesters. Certainly yellowhammers and dunnock are most usually seen in the roadside hedge. In winter fieldfares and redwing alight on the hedge, feeding on red haws and other berries. Game birds like pheasant and partridge find refuge in hedges. The vertical pattern typical of woodland wildlife (see p. 110) is in fact reproduced, and can easily be demonstrated, in a local hedge.

Since hedgerows are easily accessible alongside roads and paths they are ideal sites for environmental studies by handicapped children. A wheelchair has only to be set alongside a hedge, and the pupil is at once in close contact with woodland species.

A hedgerow survey

While it is not always possible to determine the age of a hedgerow by historical means, it has been calculated that an approximate estimation can be made by counting the numbers of different trees and shrubs in a distance of thirty yards (metres). Walk thirty good paces, count the tree species, and the age of the hedgerow is this number × 100 years. Thus, in my own hedge at the rear of the garden I have some ash, oak and several hawthorn in that given distance and consequently the hedge should date back about 300 years to the seventeenth century. Likewise a hedge with ten species or more in the measured stretch probably goes back to the time of the Norman Conquest. Clearly greater accuracy will be obtained by taking several samples of thirty metres in the same hedgerow.

In a recent national survey organised for school children, survey sheets were sent out asking for details of local hedges: their management; trees and shrubs present in a thirty-metre length; the age, if known; and type of soil. Further surveys are required, and sheets can be obtained from the Nature Conservancy (see Resources list). The preliminary results indicated that the birds nesting in a particular hedge depended in part on the management of the hedge and in part on the variety of shrubs present. Also, that the number of kinds of shrubs present in a thirty-metre length depends on management, soil and age. In general a hedge 100 years old has only one or two species; a hedge 200 years old has two or three species; and so on until a hedge of 1000 years existence has ten or twelve species.

For your own comparison you could select a parish boundary hedge for great age, and a garden hedge to represent a much younger one. Map the hedges by measuring or estimating the height and width, and describing the shrubs and trees you find. Different geographical areas have very different types of hedge. Those of Cornwall and Devon are in fact high walls of local stone capped with turf, the whole covered in rich plant life. The upper section includes many large trees and shrubs – oak, ash, elm, holly, hazel and many more. In south-east England the hedge is more likely to consist of rows of shrub species such as hazel or hawthorn, with occasional tall trees such as ash, and bramble, rose or sloe forming a dense tangle in the lower levels, with a grass verge on the roadside. The map produced should reflect hedge type: vertical pattern of trees, shrubs and flowering plants and approximate size.

Record all species of plant life, noting lichens, mosses and ferns by their variety if identification is impossible. Observe the hedge over longer periods for mammals and birds, setting live traps for small mammals. Insects, snails, spiders and other non-backboned species should be collected. In this way a total picture of *biological diversity* can be obtained. Collection methods are the same as for woodland animal life (see chapter 4).

Detailed study of one section of the hedge can be made by taking a *transect* from top to bottom. This may be a *line transect*, where all plants found on one vertical line down the hedgebank

	1 2 3 4 5 6 7 8 9 10
oak	x x
hazel	x x x
primrose (P)	x x x x
bluebell (B)	x x x
wood anemone (A)	x x x x
wood sorrel (S)	x
celandine (C)	x x x
grass sp. (G)	x x x x

Fig. 3.15   A survey of plants by a line transect down a hedgebank

are recorded. If the line is a long one, plants can be recorded at regular intervals along the length. Several lines can be taken to give greater accuracy, and the results set out in a table.

Alternatively all plants between two adjacent lines can be recorded in a *belt transect*. The belt is usually one yard (metre) wide and plants may be mapped by area or recorded as individuals.

Finally the hedges in a given area can be mapped on a large wall display. The area surveyed could be a parish, estate, routes

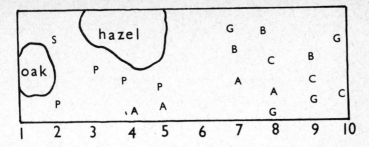

Fig. 3.16 A survey of plants by a belt transect down a hedgebank

about the school or home or any other suitable location. Give each hedge an estimation of biological diversity, calculated from the number of trees, shrubs, wild flowers, non-flowering plants and animals present. Thus, a very rich hedge can be rated '5-star' and mapped in red, the least productive hedge rated '1-star' and mapped in yellow.

The hedgerow study can be as simple or involved as you want to make it, but it is a very suitable basis for introducing study methods and a variety of subject disciplines.

4 WOODLANDS

Introduction

Woodland heritage

The plant world – flowerless plants

The floral year

Woodland variety – soils

Forests and forestry

Woodland animals

Mammals of the wood

Insects in a tree

Insect galls

4 WOODLANDS

Introduction

As we leave the town behind, we are likely to encounter woodland of one sort or another. The British landscape is rich in woodland, yet very little is natural and much has been planted in this century. After surveying the history of our woodland scene, and the impact of man, we shall investigate the world of plants, both flowering plants and lower plants. A number of projects follow, which can be undertaken by children of all abilities. There are collections to make and surveys to draw up in your local wood. Soil is important to woodland development, so we describe a variety of experiments for class and home in this section. We look at the growth of British forestry in recent years and at the work of the forester. Finally, we shall study the rich animal life in our woods, especially the mammals and insects, and see how to carry out our own studies in both short and long-term projects. Night watching at badger setts, live-trapping of small mice and voles and collecting insect galls are all activities the handicapped young person can enjoy in a woodland environment.

Woodland heritage

Britain has always been largely naturally wooded – oak in England and pine in Scotland – and trees are an important feature of our landscape. The story of our woods is a long one, it goes back to the period of the Ice Ages when Britain like much of the northern world was covered by great glaciers extending from the Arctic regions. As the climate became warmer and the ice retreated our vegetation was joined by plants from more southerly countries, untouched by the ice. Tundra at first covered our lands: prostrate shrubby plants of bilberry and cowberry, typical of modern moors, grew amid lichens and mosses, clinging to rocks and gaining some protection from

small stunted bushes of willow and birch. As years passed and
the climate improved, trees advanced north to colonise dry
ground with forests of birch and pine. Wet low-lying ground
became covered by willow woodland and Britain began its
history as a wooded landscape. Gradually trees such as hazel,
oak, elm, lime and alder appeared from the Continent of
Europe, to be followed by ash, beech and hornbeam. Some
flourished while others declined: oak, ash and hazel have always
been successful in our landscape, while lime, hornbeam and
beech are less numerous in our natural woodlands. Today our
commonest native trees are oak, ash, birch, willow and alder.
Although the pine survived for two thousand years as the
dominant tree in the dry Boreal climate after the retreat of the
ice sheets, it eventually retained a stronghold only in the great
pine covering much of Scotland. Today only fragments remain
to tell the story of our woodland history.

Britain's woodland has been important to man throughout
our history. With the arrival of our first farmers from the
Continent in the New Stone Age some five thousand years ago,
trees were felled to create the land needed for planting and
grazing, and so began the destruction of our great oak woods.
Regeneration of woodland by seedling growth was prevented by
animals foraging among the trees, so no new trees grew up to
replace the ones that had been lost. As man and his livestock
increased, the forest dwindled. With the advent of metals,
bronze and iron, man's tools improved and forest clearance
continued at a greater rate. By the end of the Bronze Age all the
hills of southern England had been cleared of trees and become
grassland – the now familiar downs. The climate was now dryer
and the downs less suitable for tree growth. During the
succeeding Iron Age the climate once again turned wet, and oak
forests grew vigorously, but against the much improved iron
axes and iron ploughs forests continued to change for farmland.
Romans, Saxons, Danes, all depleted the forest so that by the
time of the Doomsday survey (1086) four-fifths of Britain's
forests had gone. All that remained were patches of woodland
among fields.

In the Middle Ages forests were protected by Kings for
hunting, but by Tudor times the country began to appreciate its
great loss of building timber – for furniture, houses and

especially ships. Large size, good quality oaks were needed to increase the English fleet and many majestic trees were lost. Wood too was required for the ever-demanding smelting furnaces of the growing iron industry. The fuel used was charcoal, which burns with twice the heat of burning wood. Trees were felled, chopped and reduced to charcoal by burning the wood with limited air supply. Fortunately for our woods coke was eventually found to be a more efficient fuel and in the eighteenth century the metal industries moved to the great coalfields.

Landscaped parkland was a feature of this period, as wealth increased and there was much new planting, often with exotic species introduced from abroad. Beech woods and driveways were established and the grounds of many large and famous houses, which we can still see today, came under the influence of notable landscape designers.

In more recent years the need for timber led to the establishment of the Forestry Commission, with a definite planting policy based on economic returns. Fast-growing trees were preferred to native species and conifer plantations appeared in upland and hilly districts. Agricultural fertile land was still needed for food production but any area of wet peat moorland could be drained and planted. Spruce, larch, fir and pine became more familiar to the eye than oak, ash and elm, and with this change in woodland there came a change in wildlife. The forest area of today is only a small fraction of that in the New Stone Age, when our story of man and trees began, but that which remains has still an important part to play in our lives.

The plant world – flowerless plants

There is no better way to introduce a child to the plant world than to take a woodland walk. There is sensuous delight in kicking through fallen leaves in autumn and winter, in the crackle of branches as they break under foot, in the sensation of entering a dark forest. And towering trees, wild flowers in the spring, ferns in dark glades, moss carpets across the ground, autumn toadstools constitute a complete plant kingdom under one leafy roof. A visit to a local wood should become one of the most exciting events in the year of any child, and to follow a woodland through its own changing year is a great educational experience.

During much of the year, especially from late summer until spring, there are few flowers to be seen in the woodland, yet it is still alive and full of interest.

Lichens, fungi, mosses, liverworts and ferns are all there to find and many are especially attractive when examined under a lens or microscope. Most flowerless plants form suitable material for collections and simple projects at home. They can be kept alive and flourishing on a small layer of damp soil in glass or polythene containers fitted with a lid to retain humid conditions. In such a container your own woodland system can be designed and grown. On the other hand lichens and mosses are best kept permanently by drying them in air and storing them in separate packets or small envelopes. The transparent packets in which you buy stamps are especially suitable and can be purchased from a good philatelic shop. Each specimen should be labelled with details of the habitat or situation in which it was found (e.g. on soil, damp wood, rotting tree trunk), the locality and date. When you have identified your plant the name can be added. Larger specimens and lichens on rocks or bark can be glued on to index cards and stored in a box.

Mushrooms and toadstools

In autumn when the wood is cool and damp, but before frosts arrive, you can find many different kinds of mushrooms and toadstools growing in the wood. They belong to the group of plants called fungi, and are great fun to observe and collect. The fungi which you bring home from a woodland walk are best carried in an old basket where they can be laid carefully without damage – in polythene bags they sweat and are easily broken. With toadstools you can create a miniature 'fungal garden' on a kitchen tray or a large flat dish. Landscape your garden with pieces of decaying wood, mosses, lichens and decomposing leaf litter. Place the fungi in small pockets to create a living effect. Try to make a picture or painting of your garden. You may be able to keep everything fresh overnight by covering the whole tray with a polythene bag. However, some are POISONOUS and should not be eaten, so your hands must be well washed after handling them. Fungi are of many colours, often bright reds, purple, brown or yellow, by which you can be helped to

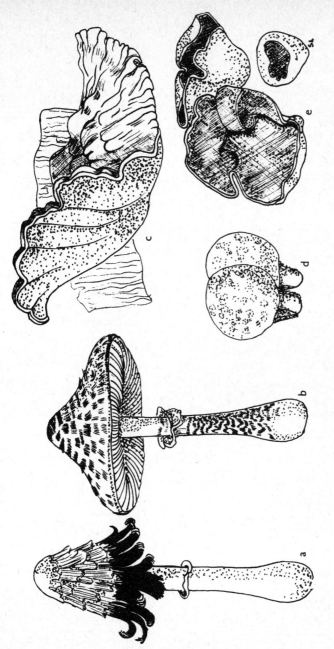

Fig. 4.1 Woodland fungi a. ink cap b. parasol c. bracket fungus d. puff balls e. orange peel cup fungus

identify them. There are a number of well illustrated books for reference. Fungi differ from all other plants in that they contain no *chlorophyll* and thus do not manufacture their own foods; they live on damp and decaying plant and animal matter such as rotting leaves and wood, dung and even animal carcasses. In this way fungi play an important role in the wood, decomposing dead matter which otherwise would accumulate, and returning much needed food substances (*nutrients*) to the soil where they

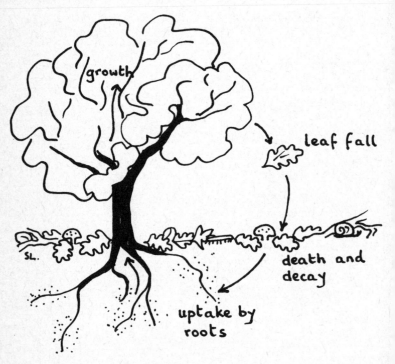

Fig. 4.2 A woodland nutrient cycle

can be used again by the other plants. Some fungi are parasites growing at the expense of other living organisms, but these are usually microscopic. All fungi have numerous branching white threads (*hyphae*) growing through their food material or the soil, and only at certain times of the year, usually autumn, do they produce the familiar mushroom form which contains thousands of minute spores. These are released from between the gills on the underside of the mushroom cap and may be blown by the wind or carried by insects to establish new fungal growths elsewhere.

Making a spore print – take home a fresh toadstool and cut the cap from the stem taking care to avoid any damage. Place the cap, gillside downwards, on a piece of black paper (some fungi produce black spores and then white paper must be used). Cover the cap with a jam jar or suitable container to retain moisture and leave overnight. When you lift the cap carefully, a print will be left behind, formed by the spores dropping from the gills. This can be covered by clear self-adhesive plastic (for covering books) purchased from any good stationer. The finished print can be mounted in an exercise book or scrap book next to a drawing or photograph of the complete fungus, and you can add details about the habitat, locality and date. In time you will have your own 'Toadstool book' about the fungi in your favourite wood.

Lichens
Branches of trees are often densely covered by grey-green plant growths which appear dry and often dead. These are lichens,

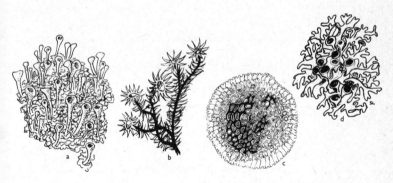

Fig. 4.3 Lichens of woods and walls: a. *Cladonia fimbriata* b. *Usnea florida* c. *Lecanora muralis* d. *Hypogynia physodes*

whose plant body is really formed from two plants growing together as one: the body or *thallus* is made up of fungal threads (*hyphae*) which provide water and anchorage, together with simple green algal cells which manufacture food substances.

Thus the lichen can grow where no other plants grow. Many encrust rock or stone surfaces; others have a leafy growth from growing over soil, wood or stone surface; some branch profusely and are attached by a single holdfast to their substrate. Brightly coloured red cups sometimes adorn the lichen surface, or a red swelling may grow at the end of a tube. These are spore producing structures and enable the plant to spread. Other lichens have scattered warty growths over their surface: black, yellow, red, green, orange and a variety of other colours. All produce spores which disperse the plants throughout the habitat. Their abundance in a wood or on an old stone wall is indicative of their success.

Mosses and liverworts

Everyone recognises a moss growing on the garden wall, on the roof, on greenhouse soil or in cracks between the paving stones.

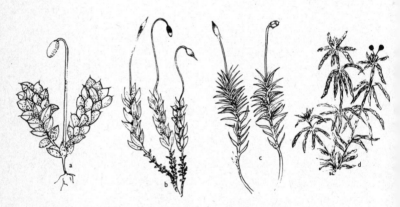

Fig. 4.4   Mosses of woods and walls: a. *Bryum*   b. *Mnium*   c. *Polytrichum*   d. *Sphagnum*

On the other hand very few people recognise the carpets of lush green liverworts growing on a damp woodland bank or beside a stream flowing through a local wood. The two plants are related, however, having similar spore producing structures, and form a group of flowerless plants known as *Bryophytes*.

Mosses have stems covered with very small leaves which require microscopic examination to identify them. At different times of the year long brown stems arise which bear a capsule, from which spores will suddenly be released and borne by the wind to grow elsewhere. Thus a new carpet of green moss becomes established, holding in the water so necessary for growth of the seedlings of higher plants. Mosses are, therefore, the first colonisers of bare surfaces – burned ground, felled woodland or mountain scree slopes.

Liverworts by contrast grow in wet places, their large leafy outgrowths closely covering the soil surface, attached by numerous white root-like rhizoids. Small buds which fall away and grow into new plants may be produced on the leafy surface of the parent plant. At certain times capsules from which spores are released grow on slender stalks above the plant body.

Ferns

The most complex and advanced flowerless plants to see in the woods are ferns. They love shady damp conditions and their

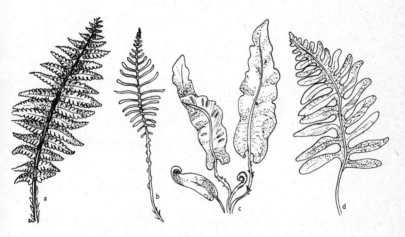

Fig. 4.5 Woodland ferns: a. Male fern   b. Hard fern   c. Hart's tongue   d. Polypody

leafy fronds can reach heights of several feet. The frond is formed by many leaflets (*pinnae*) which branch again into numerous pinnules. A single fern frond can be collected and a rubbing made on paper with a wax crayon. The entire frond can be mounted on a large sheet of paper after drying and pressing beneath newspaper. The underside of each pinnule has numer-

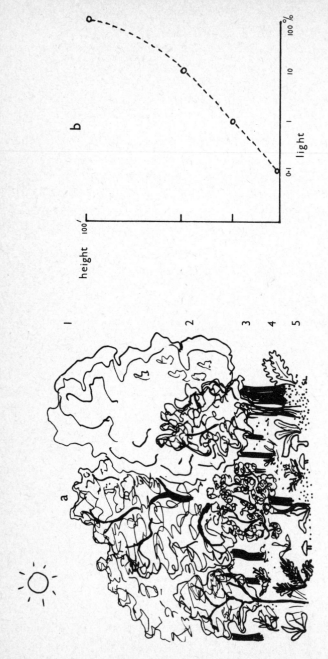

Fig. 4.6   Woodland structure and pattern: a. Vertical layering in a wood 1) upper canopy   2) lower canopy
3) shrub layer   4) herb layer   5) ground layer; b. the decline in light availability from canopy to
ground level

ous clusters of spores which are released when the spore case bursts. You can try to grow small fern plants from their spores on damp soil or peat kept in a small glass or plastic box with a lid. Shake the ripe brown spores on to the soil and leave in a light place. The lid will retain the humid conditions necessary. Germination is slow and you must leave them for several months before you will notice the young plants.

The floral year

In woods in mid-summer, you will probably not find many wild flowers in flower. This is because the dense leafy canopy of the trees filters out much of the light before it reaches the woodland floor – you will notice how dark and cool it suddenly becomes when you enter the wood, away from the reach of the sun. Water and food substances may also be in short supply in the soil, since the trees are growing most rapidly at this season and leaving little for the softer herbaceous plants. So the edges of the wood, or open glades and rides may be the best places to search for your flowers – there they still receive enough sunlight for growth and may flower over longer periods. These are also often the easiest places to take the person confined to a wheelchair.

A visit to the wood in spring and early summer shows the natural flowering season for our common woodland plants, snowdrops, primrose and bluebells, but we should notice that these do not all flower or produce their leaves at the same time.

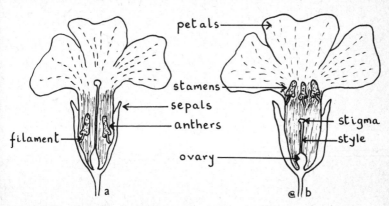

Fig. 4.7 Variation between primroses: a. pin-eye b. thrum-eye

The tree canopy is still open at this period, since their leaves do not appear until later in the year. The shade phase of beech, oak and ash woods covers mainly the months of May until October – so spring flowers take advantage of the light and growing conditions. This is particularly true in beech woods growing on richly nutrient soils. The dense beech canopy allows little light through (5 per cent) compared with the oak (20 per cent). Few shrubs can grow in dense beech woods, except evergreens such as holly and yew, which grow throughout the year, often in low light conditions. The spring wild flowers include snowdrops, wood anemones, celandines, primroses, wood sorrel and bluebells. In mid-summer a few rare orchids may grow among

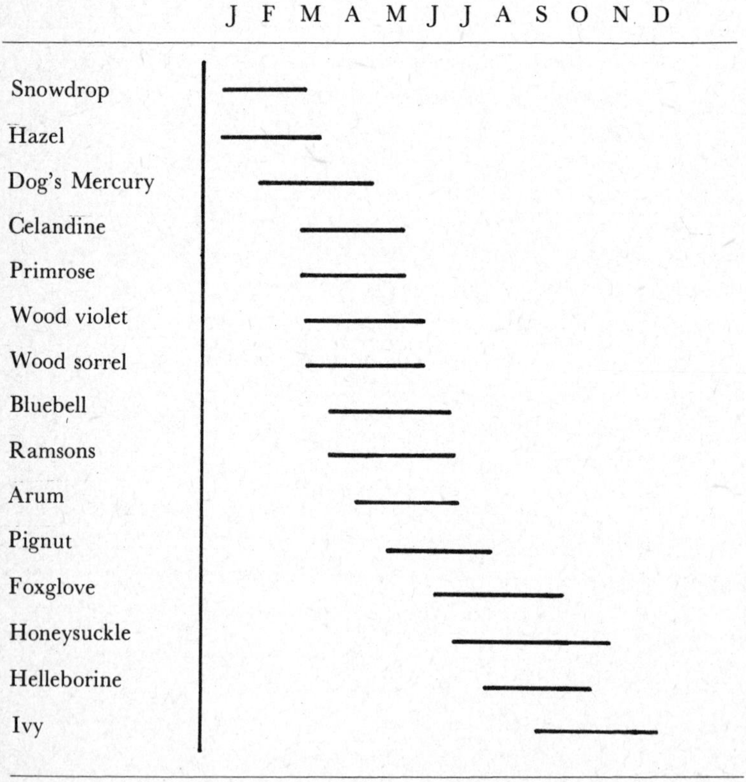

Fig. 4.8   The flowering year of some woodland plants

the beech: helleborines, twayblade or the strange birdsnest orchid, feeding on rotting leaves with the aid of a fungus partner.

Ash trees, with their more open compound leaves allow plenty of light to reach the floor, on the other hand do not become shady until June, so have a wealth of wild flowers growing beneath the trees in early summer: meadowsweet, hemp agrimony and enchanter's nightshade, as well as good shrub growth of elder, alder and buckthorn.

Oak woods develop on both poor and rich soils and the ground flora varies accordingly. Leaves are late to open, often into June, and the light plentiful. Shrubs can grow profusely, hazel, elder, honeysuckle and wild flowers abound.

Making a flower collection

At some time in their life most children enjoy collecting wild flowers, and if this is done over a long period the collection can become extensive in species and form your own herbarium. Identification should be made using leaves as well as the flower, and only a single flower should be taken. The plant must never be dug up since this is illegal, and it will be there for others to see at a later time. Do not pick rare flowers such as orchids.

The flower can be dried and pressed flat in a small flower press made from two pieces of board. Newspaper should separate each flower, and the outer boards held tightly together with straps or a belt. More simply a number of heavy books can be used to press down on your flowers laid between newspaper. After a few days the flower can be mounted on a sheet of paper or in a scrap book. Small pieces of sellotape will fix the specimen in position. A better result can be obtained by mounting the flower on card beneath self-adhesive plastic sheeting. In this way it can be handled easily without worry about damage. The collection can be arranged around different places you visit – the garden, a hedge or a wood. But remember that colours tend to fade and pressed flowers never look quite like the fresh plant.

A flower diary can be kept at the same time, recording the plants you see in different months in each locality. You will be surprised at how long the list becomes over a year, for you should certainly see several hundred different wild flowers.

A word about identification. There are many good flower

books with excellent illustrations for children and adults, but no *small* book can hope to cover all the flowers seen in a variety of habitats throughout the year. It can be frustrating to both the child and parent not to be able to find in a new book the flower you brought home that day and this frustration can lead to a sense of failure in a very rewarding pastime. Consequently, I feel that it is very important to obtain a good comprehensive field guide from a popular series, which illustrates most species in colour. A small book from one of the children's series can be used alongside this one, so that the young person can make her or his own comparisons between pictures and specimens and practise identification.

Woodland variety – soils
Most British woodlands have a mixed range of trees growing in them, although certain species of trees are more likely to

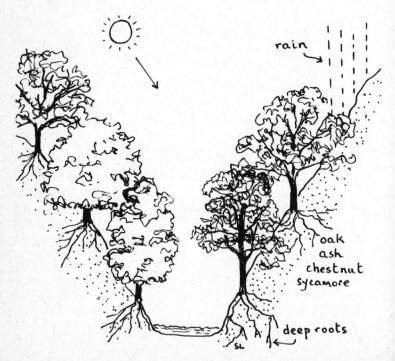

rain

oak
ash
chestnut
sycamore

deep roots

SL

Fig. 4.9 Mixed valley woodland

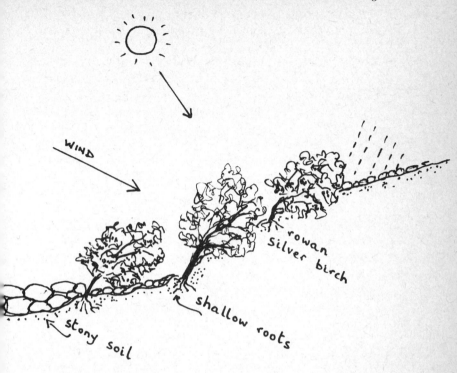

Fig. 4.10   Hillside wood

produce woodland than others. A number of factors determine where trees grow naturally and why you are more likely to find a dense oak wood in a river valley than on the side of a mountain. The shape of the ground is especially important, affecting soil depth and stability. The ground slope determines drainage, and the aspect – south or north facing for instance – the amount of light reaching the wood, the temperature and wind effects. All of these 'climatic' factors determine the species and growth of trees. Soils vary in different areas of the country and are related to the nature of the underlying rock. Thus, limestone, chalk and granite produce very different soils which in turn encourage the establishment of different types of woodland. The oak grows widely on many soil types, rich and poor, but the ash prefers soil rich in lime. Beech grows well on well drained shallow soils while birch can colonise the shallow stony unstable soils of mountainsides. Alders and willows tolerate wet, water-logged soils rich in nutrients near rivers and in fenland.

Although the soil plays a significant role in determining tree growth, trees in turn play their part in determining the soil structure. Soil is only in part formed by weathering of the rocks; the decomposition of leaves, twigs and branches adds greatly to its quality. Fungi and micro-organisms assist soil animals in this breakdown of plant matter to form the humus content of the soil, and where there is great activity by earthworms and other fauna the humus rapidly becomes mixed with the deeper mineral sub-soils. This results in the characteristic soil type ('brown earth') of rich deciduous woods. By contrast soils beneath dense conifer stands (pine, spruce, fir) produce poor acid soils with little activity by microbes (bacteria) and few soil animals. Fungi alone attack the hard resinous leaves on the forest floor and the mouldy smell and presence of white fungal strands can be distinguished in a handful of rotting pine needles. The humus is therefore slow to form and stays as a distinct layer, dark in colour, above the mineral soil. Beneath the humus layer there is often a pale region where the plant nutrients have been washed out by the products of humus decomposition, only to be re-

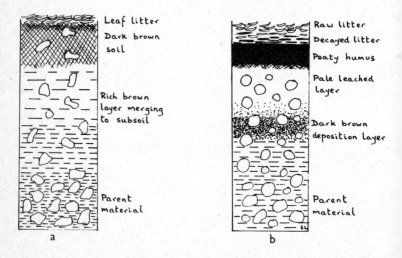

Fig. 4.11   Soil profiles: a. brown earth (mixed woodland)   b. podsol (conifer woodland)

deposited deeper in the soil. Such a soil type or *podsol* has distinct zones or 'horizons' which can be seen by digging a vertical profile in the woodland floor.

Simple experiments with soil
Any of the following experiments can be made with soil collected from the garden, woods, moors, dunes or other habitats visited. It is best to compare different soils.

The constituents of soil
1. Place a small cupful of soil in water in a tall glass jar (a coffee jar or old milk bottle) and shake vigorously. Add a little sodium carbonate (from a chemist) to the water. Gravel, coarse sand and fine sand settle almost at once. Silt and clay are slower to settle and fine clay particles remain suspended, clouding the water, for many days. Humus materials may remain floating at the surface. Measure each layer with a ruler and draw the final results in bands on graph paper (or narrow-lined paper). Repeat for different soils, using the same containers and amount of soil.

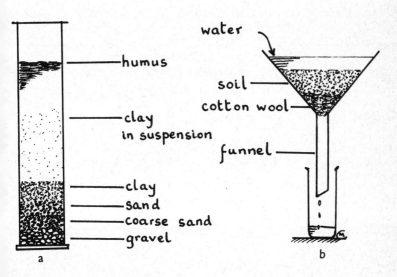

Fig. 4.12 Some experiments with soil: a. separation of layers b. soil drainage

2. Take a known amount of soil (use the same cup) and dry it in the room on a sheet of newspaper. Rub it by hand until broken and loose in texture. Sieve the dry soil through meshes of different sizes. First use a wide mesh garden sieve or plastic kitchen colander to remove stones and gravel (part one). Then, pass the rest through a metal flour sieve (part two) and finally through a plastic flour sieve or teastrainer (part three). That which passes through the finest mesh (part four) contains mainly clay and fine sand. Each portion can now be weighed on fine kitchen scales (or a spring balance if you have one). The results can be given in a table or simple diagram.

3. Take a small quantity of dry soil on a teaspoon and place in a suitable glass container (a very small bottle for food colouring materials). Add enough hydrogen peroxide to cover the soil and *warm slightly* in a pan of water placed on the cooker; do not boil the water but simply allow the soil in the peroxide to froth. When frothing has ceased remove the glass container from the pan and pour water down the sides to wash the material back to the bottom. The humus in the soil is destroyed by the peroxide and on settling the soil appears much paler in colour. It is the humus that gives soil its rich black colour. *SAFETY* Take care, since hydrogen peroxide can damage the skin and eyes. For this reason the experiment may be best demonstrated by an adult to the child.

Soil drainage

4. Take a filter funnel such as one used for wine-making or for pouring oil (obtainable from an ironmonger or large chain store) and place a loose plug of cotton wool inside. Half fill with a known amount of soil fairly tightly. Pour a cup of water on to the soil and measure the time it takes for all the water to drain through. Repeat with other, different soils. Sandy soils drain more rapidly than clay soils due to the larger size of soil particles in the former.

5. Repeat the last experiment and catch all the water draining through the soil. Measure the volume passing through in a plastic measuring cylinder and compare with the initial volume poured on to the soil. How much has each soil retained?

Soil water

6. Since different soils retain varying amounts of water you can

record the water content of fresh soils collected on a dry day. Weigh a known amount of soil on the kitchen scales (say 250gms. or half-pound). Place on an old tin tray or lid in the oven and allow to dry for a short time at just over 100°C. This is a *very low* setting and should not be raised to hasten the process. When the soil is totally dry remove and cool. Reweigh and calculate the difference in weight. The difference represents, the water contained in that soil. What percentage of the fresh soil was water? Do the same experiment with several different types of soil? Which types of soil contain most water?

Soil reaction
7. Some soils have a high content of lime or chalk and are called 'alkaline'; others have a high peat content and are called 'acidic'. Most soils have a balance somewhere between the two extremes and are almost 'neutral'. In order to measure the degree of acidity/alkalinity in a soil you can try a variety of tests. Garden supply shops will supply test papers which change colour slightly when in contact with the soil, which must first be made into a solution in pure water (distilled or rainwater). In large cities rainwater itself is often acidic and distilled water must be used (this can be obtained at a garage). The change in colour is compared with a colour chart to tell you the degree of alkalinity or acidity.

The presence of quantities of lime in a soil can be demonstrated by adding a little acid (e.g. vinegar) to the soil and observing the frothing reaction (effervescence) which occurs.

Soil animals and decomposition
8. Fill a nylon net fruit bag with some fresh leaf litter. Bury it in the garden and mark the position well. Leave from autumn until spring. Recover your bag and note any decomposition of the leaves. Replace and leave for the year. Does the litter break down into soil? Do many soil animals feed on the leaves? Try the same experiment with a bag of fine mesh – a pair of tights or muslin will be suitable. Which sample of litter rots more quickly?

Forests and forestry
Pines, spruces and larches (conifers) are favoured by foresters because they grow faster than broad-leaved trees and produce

straight timber. They can grow on poor, often acid soils and from high peat moorland to coastal sand dunes, ground which otherwise might be thought of little economic use to man. It is now easier to find an evergreen conifer forest than a native piece of oak woodland. Three species of conifer are however native in the British Isles: the Scots Pine, which was once widely distributed in post-glacial times and found its stronghold throughout the highlands and lowlands of Scotland; the Juniper, which is also seen among these pine forests, but grows also in the Lake District and chalk Downs of south-east England; and the Yew, our third native conifer and perhaps the most famous, which can attain ages greater than any other – some trees are reputed to be over a thousand years old. One such tree in a Surrey churchyard measures 45 feet (14 metres) in diameter and has an estimated age of 2,500 years. Yew grows naturally on chalk soils, especially in southern England, but forms a good shrub or under-canopy growth in beech woods.

When the Forestry Commission was established in 1919 British forests were much depleted and it was considered that conifers growing naturally on the Continent would be best to introduce for the production of timber. This led to much planting of European Larch, Norway Spruce ('Christmas tree') and our own Scots Pine. But our climate is cooler and moister than that of much of Europe and our spring frosts did not help growth of young trees and shrubs. Harsh Continental winters, when the tree lies dormant, are followed by a more reliable spring and summer. So the search for our new forest conifers was spread wider afield to the west coast of North America which has a similar damp climate. Sitka spruce was introduced to flourish on wet acid moors in northern Britain. This has a Christmas tree appearance but the needles are green above and bluish underneath. The timber it produces is used mainly for making paper. The Western Hemlock, Western Red Cedar, Redwood (*Sequoia*), Douglas Fir and Monterey Pine, which can all be found in our plantations, were likewise brought from western North America to grow alongside larches from Japan.

In this way the cosmopolitan nature of our forests was established, which has lent them a particular educational value. Forest trails can be found in many regions of this country, with illustrated leaflets giving details of the trees encountered on your

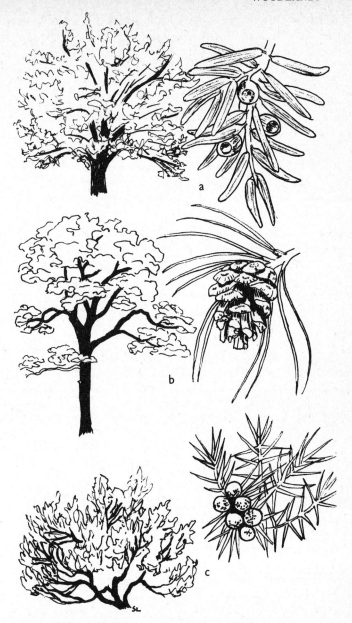

Fig. 4.13   British native conifers: a. Yew   b. Scots Pine
c. Juniper

walk. The Forestry Commission can supply a list of such trails and many parts are suitable for wheelchairs, even though the going may be a little rough at times. There are several simple guides to conifers providing colour illustrations of the tree, leaves and cones.

Cones, which characterise all conifers, bear the flowers of the tree; some are male and others female, and it is the dry female cones in which the seeds ripen that can be found lying beneath the tree. The cones of the pine open in dry warm weather to release the seeds. They stay on the tree for one or two years before ripening, and even after release of the seeds may remain there. Cones are ideal for a collection since they are dry, easily stored and can be used to identify the tree.

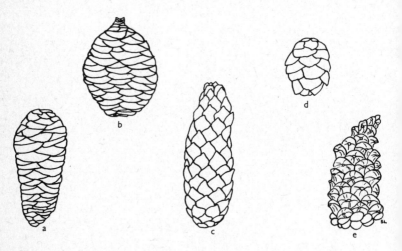

Fig. 4.14 Collecting cones: a. Fir b. Cedar c. Spruce d. Larch e. Pine

A visit to a tree nursery may also be possible, to see how young conifers are grown from seeds until they are about ½ metre high and ready to be planted out. In some moorland districts the new afforestation schemes are still in progress, and often young conifers can be seen planted to landscape a development such as a reservoir or motorway. Derelict areas, with industrial waste tips, might likewise be planted to give a more pleasing environment. Different situations demand different planting techniques, but extensive plantations on wet upland moors involve land drainage followed by ploughing. The young trees are planted in the raised ridges and the furrows provide further drainage around the roots, for conifers do not grow well when the soil is waterlogged. Chemical fertilisers are added to encourage growth. As the plantation matures and the leafy canopy closes together, so the forest becomes dark and few plants are found on the ground level. Poor thin trees are removed regularly to give more light and room for the stronger ones. The 'thinnings' are used for fence poles and paper pulp. The forest develops and 'rides' are cleared between areas of trees to form a road system for access by tractors to the trees and to act as firebreaks. Fire is the forester's worst enemy and can devastate a mature forest in a short time. Pests too, such as the caterpillar of the pine looper moth, can completely defoliate a forest in a growing season and cause economic loss, so aerial spraying may be done by a helicopter or small plane to treat with pesticides against fungi, insects, or even weeds in a younger plantation.

Eventually the trees are ready to fell, but usually the forest will be felled one part at a time. This prevents too dramatic a change to the environment, and erosion of the soil by rainfall once the roots of the trees are not there to hold the soil together. New planting in an area recently felled will ultimately replace those trees removed for timber, and so the cycle continues. It is a long cycle, lasting about seventy years for conifers, though most trees are removed before they reach maturity at about twenty or thirty years.

There is a great deal to interest the child in watching the forester at work, whether in a large conifer plantation or in an estate woodland. The noise of the powersaw, the large machinery to drag away felled trees and the sawmill at the end of the process all help tell the total story of a forest. Recently the Forestry Commission has seen the potential of forests not only for timber production but also for recreation. Nature trails, horse rides, camp sites and picnic areas are some of the pleasures they can offer, and new plantations are often better landscaped than in the past, with fringe planting of broad-leaved trees, so that it merges more naturally into the local scenery. Wildlife is further encouraged in this way, adding to the interest created by the forest. There are nevertheless few forests managed for timber that cannot be improved as wildlife habitats.

Woodland Animals

Many of the animals that we see in our parks and gardens are, in fact woodland creatures. As woods and forests were cleared, so animals moved in search of a new place to live, many developing an association with man. The ancestors of the grey squirrel, field mouse, hedgehog and mole commonly seen in gardens, even in city centres, came from the woods. Our garden birds can all still be found on a woodland walk, although the forest may at first seem to you a dead and deserted place. There is a wealth of wildlife seeking shelter among the trees, living at every conceivable level in the woodland community. In the higher branches among the leafy canopy rooks and wood pigeons nest, while in the dense conifer plantations the minute goldcrest flits and makes his high pitched call. Woodpeckers and tree-creepers search the tree trunks for insects and different tits seek holes in which to nest. Owls move at night hunting for the many small mammals scurrying across the woodland floor. In the shrubs of elder, hazel, holly and hawthorn blackbirds and thrushes sing their dawn songs and feed on ripe berries, while pheasant and woodcock move amongst the dead leaf litter, their brown mottled plumage giving camouflage from man and his gun. Each species has its specific living and feeding position (*a niche*) in the community, forming an interdependent pattern, rather than the 'struggle for existence' that would follow if all competed for the same space and food.

Mammals of the wood

Searching for mammals can be difficult, so many of us have never observed wild badgers and deer, or even seen a fox prowling by day or night. Yet they are there to be seen; with patience you may watch squirrel and hedgehog, fox and badger and other woodland creatures. Mammals often live secret lives underground and appear only at dusk to feed and play under the protection of darkness. Their special senses are well developed: large eyes and ears and long whiskers are all adaptations to inform them of the presence of danger.

A few mammals are active in full daylight. Squirrels may be

seen moving among the branches and can become tame enough to associate with man. Shrews must feed regularly and search for earthworms and insects constantly, since they require to eat their own weight in food every four hours. Fallow and roe deer may be spotted among the trees, grazing in small herds, but at the slightest noise or movement they are away, bounding into the deeper parts of the forest. Rabbits too graze, but more often at the woodland edge where the grass is lush and the soil deeper for digging the warren, away from the problem of roots. So the mammals are there, playing an essential role in the life of the community, but we need to look carefully for their signs.

Making a plaster cast of tracks –

Tracks can be found, especially where the forest floor is damp and muddy, at the side of a river or stream where woodland animals stop to drink, or at the entrance to holes and lairs where the soil has been disturbed. Footprints are quite distinctive and there are several books available with illustrations to identify them by. You can make a permanent collection of tracks by making plaster casts. Make a mould with a strip of cardboard (2" wide) bent in a circle to surround the footprint. Hold the ends in position and remove any twigs or leaves carefully. Pour in the plaster of Paris (mixed with water to a creamy consistency, sufficient to give a depth of about one inch) from a small bowl or jug. Allow it to dry for 20 minutes. Lift the cast and take home in the mould to provide support. Gently remove the card and wash the mud away from the plaster under a tap. An old toothbrush can give a final scrub for more difficult parts but do it carefully when the cast is hard. Label your cast with the name of the mammal, locality and date.

Remains and droppings

Many small mammals – mice and voles – feed in a particular manner and leave traces of their presence. Chewed hazel nuts are well worth examining: squirrels, wood-mice and bank voles leave differently shaped holes and damaged shells. In conifer woods damaged cones are signs that mammals are present. Squirrels and mice both eat seeds from cones and leave their remains beneath the trees. Trees and woodland plants may themselves be damaged by mammals feeding, rubbing their antlers or scratch-

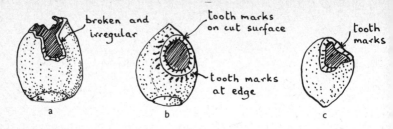

Fig. 4.15   Hazel nuts can reveal the presence of mammals: a. squirrel   b. woodmouse   c. Bank vole

ing on bark. Torn twigs and shoots, gnaw marks on trees and stripped bark are all signs of deer. Fallow are the most common in broad-leaved woods and parks, although other species such as Sika and Muntjac have become established, while roe deer are increasing in numbers in forestry plantations.

Droppings can indicate the presence of some larger mammals. Badgers live communally in setts and, having very clean habits, do not soil their own underground home. Rather they visit the surface at night to feed and deposit their droppings in one small earth scrape. If you find a number of large holes in a wood, especially on a bank surrounded by elders, this is probably a badger sett. Nettles grow near the holes on disturbed ground and fresh digging, straw bedding at the entrances, footprints and recent paths to and from the holes indicate current occupation. Search about for their dung pits close to one of the well used paths, and note whether the droppings are quite liquid or dry. Hairs can be caught on low branches or brambles, and old bones and skulls may even be found after the sett has been cleaned out in the spring. Collect all the evidence you can of badger activity and put twigs at the entrance to the holes, bedded in the soil, to find out which are most often used. Visit the sett daily for a few days – the twigs will be moved by the badgers as they come out at night. Badger-watching can be a great excitement and I have spent many an evening as dusk falls sitting beneath a tree, with camera and flash-gun, awaiting the rustle of twigs, the low grunting snuffing noises and, if very fortunate, the sight of that black and white striped head. Young badgers play, the parents lumber along their tracks or rub against a tree trunk – there is always great activity. But not every night is a success. It may rain so they don't come out, or they may gain your scent and disappear underground almost immediately. Always check the wind direction and sit down-wind of the sett, not too close, and under cover of a tree trunk. Take up a position an hour before dark and once night falls move as little as possible. Patience is the key to your success, but the final reward will be well worth the wait. During the long vigil you may also hear the hooting of owls and the cry of a fox or see a small, dark shape flit through the sky, moving among the trees in search of insects. This is a bat, another mammal, and a few species roost in old trees in holes in the branches, or in barns closeby. They are the only mammals to fly, possessing a thin, dark membrane of skin between the extended fingers and attached to the hind legs. They hunt in the darkness using radar techniques to locate any objects in their flight path and to find the moths and beetles on which they feed. By day they hang upside down, either in colonies or singly, asleep and preserving their energies. During the winter they truly hibernate, their body temperature falling low and the heart and pulse beating only once or twice a minute. Bat roosts may be traced by the remains of moth and beetle wings on the ground beneath a tree or in an old building. If the roost is an old and large one the droppings accumulate to great depths and there is a strong smell of ammonia from its decomposition. The pipistrelle is the most common bat near buildings, but in the wood the natterer's bat, whiskered and noctule may be seen, while Daubenton's bat flies low close to water.

Nature by night can be as exciting as by day and there are great rewards for the nocturnal naturalist. I have spent an enjoyable stroll along country lanes, with a group of totally deaf children, eyes alert for sights of the barn owl or bat; flashlights and Gaz-lamps at the ready to show a field mouse scuttling through a hedgebank or a hedgehog making slow progress across the road.

Trapping –

Small mammals may be caught *alive* in specially designed traps, examined and released *without any danger to the animal*. Traps are unfortunately now very expensive to purchase and difficult to make at home, but as a group activity with both mentally and physically handicapped children (and adults too!) small mammal trapping is both enjoyable and educational. The Longworth trap is made of aluminium and comes in two parts: a tunnel with trip-wire which shuts the door when knocked by the animal entering the trap, and a nest box into which is placed dry straw, hay or grass and some food (rolled or crushed oats). To trap shrews some fresh meat (chopped liver or heart) must also be added to the nest box, since shrews naturally feed on worms and insects. Traps are usually given to the children to set and lay down in a hedgerow or in a line through the wood. They must be covered with ferns, grass or leaves to give camouflage, lest they attract the attention of other creatures. A set distance between traps is best (five or ten metres) and a good pace will measure this. Number the traps 1, 2, 3 . . . and set in a sequence

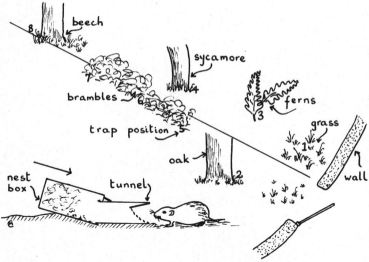

Fig. 4.16   A trap line

along a definite line. Draw a map of your area and mark the trap-line, indicating obvious markers (trees, bramble bushes, a wall) which will enable you to find each trap again. Remember that they cost a lot to buy and are going to be left out overnight. The next day things never look quite the same!

A closed door usually indicates a successful catch, though sometimes the door is sprung accidentally or a slug may have

Gone fishing

Photography for all

Professional look

In the dark room

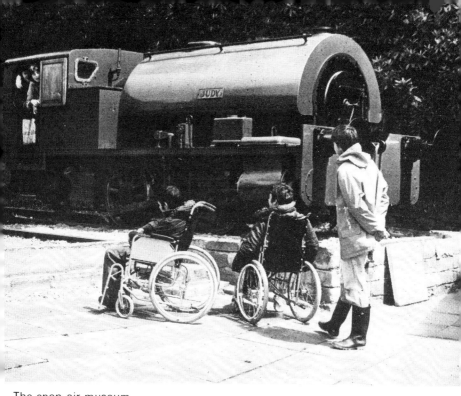

The open-air museum

History out of doors

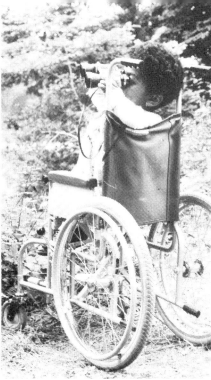

In the garden

Looking afar

A closer view

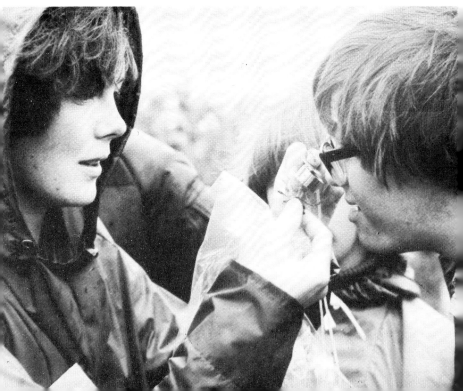

Can I touch?

Woodland walk

Measuring trees

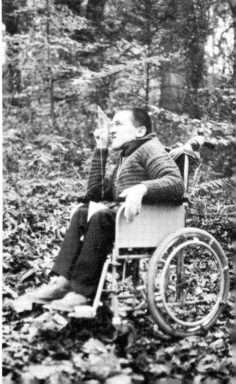

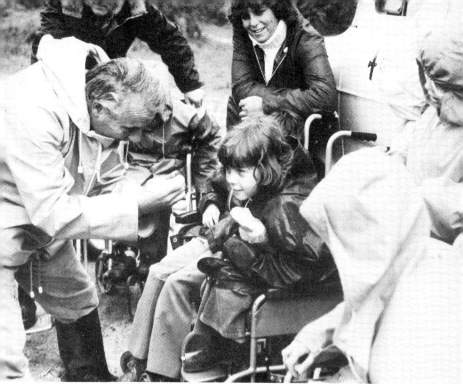

Fascination

He's rather nice

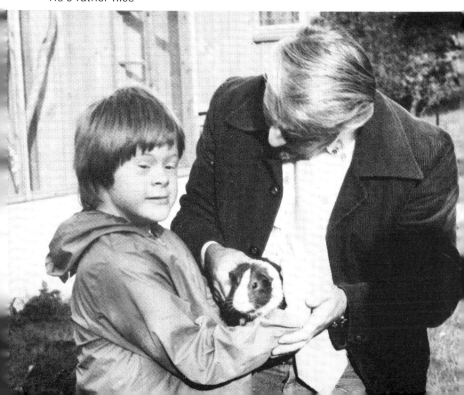

Catching weed

At the edge of the tide

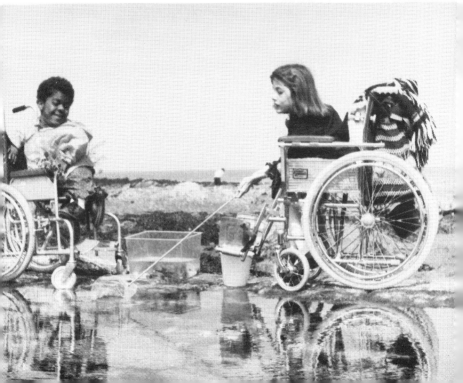

Stepping stones

Lesson on the marsh

Field work in the rain

I'm not sure

Climbing the tor

Ducks and drakes

Home made net

Among the seaweeds

Harbour holiday

Lost our way

There must be an easy way

On the Eiger

Alpine pastures

In camp

entered and tripped the wire. Chewed hay and droppings are often deposited in the tunnel and the occupied nest box smells distinctive. Empty the contents into a large steep sided container such as a white polythene washing bowl. With practice you can empty the trap by hand but it is better to see your animal clearly in a bowl before handling. Picking up should be at the base of the tail (never the tip) with the other hand holding the loose fur at the back of the neck. Mice will bite and the inevitable reaction is to let go. For short periods, the small mammal can be observed inside a polythene bag passed around the group, with each child describing one feature that he/she can observe.

The woodmouse has large, black eyes; large ears; brown fur above, white underneath; a very long tail; sharp teeth; long whiskers; long black feet; five toes but four fingers. Questions and answers about the live animal lead to a great deal of information about its habits, adaptations and life history in the wood. Mammals caught in such a way vary according to the habitat, but woodlands usually yield the woodmouse, bank vole, common shrew and perhaps pygmy shrew. By streams and rivers the larger water shrew may be caught, jet-black, shiny fur above and pale beneath. This animal can be kept in an aquarium or even a bowl of water for a few hours and observed swimming underwater, the fur trapping a layer of air. At the edge of the wood in rough grassland, or in a grassy clearing, there are often large populations of short-tailed field voles, which can cause extensive damage to young trees, especially in conifer plantations. Mice and voles should be released where they are caught, since each has a distinct territory and a female may occupy a nest close by with a litter of four or more young. In wet weather it is best not to trap, or at least to ensure that the hay stays dry in the nest box. Caught animals die more often due to hypothermia (loss of heat) than due to lack of food. If the nest box is on a downward slope, in a protected situation, with dry hay in it, there should be little threat to the animal, and after trapping one area for a long time you will find the same individuals returning time and again to the same trap.

Insects in a tree
Thousands of insects live in trees and in the leaf litter and soil

Lots of small mammals live on the reserve, in hedge-banks, long grass & brambles. Mice, Voles & Shrews are rodents, they have very alert senses and camouflaged colouring to help protect them from attack from predators. such as hawks.

You may have the chance to trap these animals using a 'Longworth' trap which is designed to keep the animals warm, well fed and ALIVE. Even if trapping is not possible, with sharp eyes you may be able to see evidence of their presence...

Gnawed seeds & nuts, tracks in wet mud or snow, nests or tunnels in long grass or just droppings.

LONG TAILED FIELD MOUSE

BANK VOLE

NEST BOX with bedding & food.
TUNNEL
BAIT
TRAP DOOR
TRIP WIRE
LONGWORTH TRAP

COMMON SHREW

Larger mammals such as rabbits and squirrels are much easier to track.

Fig. 4.17 Woodland mammals – a nature trail guide

beneath them. Many are seldom seen since they dwell in the high leafy canopy, feeding on the leaves themselves or sucking their sap by means of piercing, needle-like mouth parts. Every part of the tree is used as food, the leaves, bark, seeds and roots as well as the rotting leaves on the woodland floor. The study of insects is of great importance to the forester since many cause

FALLOW DEER

GREY SQUIRREL

FOX

RABBIT

MOLE

extensive damage to the trees and its timber, or carry diseases
such as Dutch Elm disease. We have all seen in recent years the
death of trees in the countryside due to this fungus parasite,
which is carried from one tree to another by a small bark beetle.
The female beetle bores a tunnel for her eggs beneath the bark,
at the surface of the wood. When the young larvae hatch they

make tunnels at right angles to the 'egg tunnel' where they
pupate and finally emerge as adult beetles. The tunnels are often
seen in logs bought for the fireside.

Collecting insects

Insects living among the foliage are not easy to collect since
the branches are often out of reach. Select one with a
low branch or find suitable bushes in the shrub layer of the
wood. Hold an old umbrella upsidedown under the leaves and
beat the branch gently with a stick so as not to cause any damage
to the tree. The insects fall away into the umbrella where you
can collect them before they crawl or fly away. This method is
called 'beating'. If you have no umbrella, place a large white
sheet under the tree, but you may lose a few insects which fly
away before you catch them. Insects can be picked up by the
fingers and placed in small containers – glass or polythene tubes,
old pillboxes, matchboxes, in fact anything in which you can
enclose your insects separately. Too many in one container and
they will eat each other before you reach home and you will end
up with nothing but one large beetle! Better still make yourself a
pooter which you can use to suck small insects up from the sheet

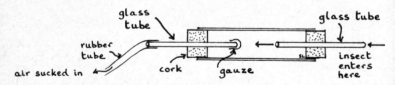

Fig. 4.18   Making a pooter

or any other surface. This prevents damage to the insect and is
operated by the mouth rather than the hands, important for
many handicapped children. Pooters can be purchased from
biological supply firms (see address list). Nets can be used to
sweep the grass and flowers beneath trees, and light nets for
catching insects such as butterflies in flight. Insects and other
animals living in the soil or dead leaves are best caught in pitfall
traps which are very easy to obtain and position. Dig a hole
beneath the tree large enough to bury a jam jar to the rim. Make
sure there is no gap between the glass rim and the soil. You have

now created a miniature 'bear trap', which will capture beetles, spiders, harvestmen, and many other members of the soil/litter fauna. Empty the jar in the morning and take home your live catch. If you must leave the trap for several days, a preservative which kills and prevents decay of the insects has to be placed in the jar. This is usually alcohol, diluted to about 50 per cent with water. Surgical spirits or methylated spirits can be used for this purpose and the insects, after sorting and examination, can be permanently stored in stronger alcohol (70 per cent). Instead of glass jam jars plastic food containers used for yoghurt, cream or salads are perfectly suitable.

Samples of the leaf litter can be taken back in polythene bags and the insects living in it collected by a 'light funnel'. Put the

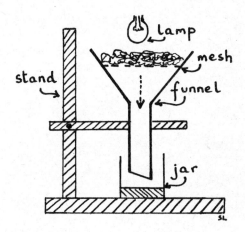

Fig. 4.19   A light funnel

leaves in a large plastic filter funnel on top of a piece of plastic garden netting or wiremesh; then place a lamp above the litter. Insects will move along from the light and heat into the cooler, damper litter beneath. Eventually they fall away, through the holes in the mesh, into a small tube or jar of alcohol. Alternatively you can catch them alive in a jam jar, but this must be emptied frequently. The funnel can be held upright by tying it to a wooden stand, which is easily made at home or in school. Many insects collected in this way help to decompose the leaves falling from trees. Woodlice, millipedes, larvae of beetles and moths all feed in this manner, while centipedes, spiders and ground beetles are the predators of the woodland floor. Smaller wingless insects – springtails and bristle-tails – living in the soil itself, are best collected by 'light funnels', and myriads of mites – a relative of the larger spider – often swarm all over the collecting jar. Watching insects and their allies is full of interest and provides opportunity to talk about the world of small creatures.

Insect galls
The familiar 'oak apple' and other abnormal growths found on that tree are plant galls, produced by the tree in response to invasion by other living organisms, usually insects. Small wingless gall wasps, only a few millimetres ($\frac{1}{4}$ inch) long, lay

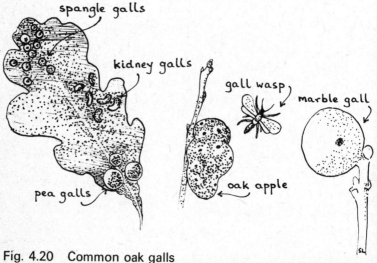

Fig. 4.20   Common oak galls

their eggs in the tree buds and in late spring the first swellings appear. By early summer the oak apple is mature, its rosy tint and fruit-like appearance giving it its common name. Inside, the grubs or larvae are hatched from the eggs but effectively sealed in chambers away from the rest of the plant, until the mature gall wasps eat their way out, leaving small round exit holes. Galls in this state are often found still attached to the tree. The insects which hatch are winged males, and females without, or with very reduced wings. After mating the females crawl down the trunk into the soil, and lay their eggs in the small roots. A new root gall appears, also rounded and berry-like. In winter the wingless females emerge, struggle to the soil surface and after surviving the perils of winter climb the trunk once again to lay eggs in the leaf buds, thus completing the cycle. The fact that these females can lay unfertilised eggs which develop successfully is a feature of gall insects.

No tree has a greater variety of insects associated with it than the oak, and many of these cause gall formation. Such galls are often easy to identify and can form a good collection, since they are dry and attached to stems, leaves or other parts of the plant. The insects living in them can easily be reared if you collect single galls, or several of the same kind, in a polythene bag and leave them for months until the adult insects emerge. These can be mounted on small pieces of card, fixed in position at the tip by a small drop of clear gum. The insects can be placed alongside their gall in a permanent collection, housed in a box with a cork base. If cork sheet is difficult to obtain, use a polystyrene ceiling tile cut to fit into the box.

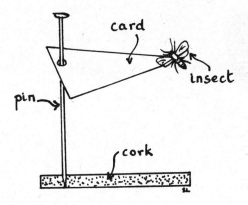

Fig. 4.21 Mounting a small insect

Oak leaves often bear small circular lens-shaped growths known as 'spangle galls' on the undersurface. When mature in autumn, they become detached from the leaves and fall to the ground. Each gall contains a larva which develops into the adult wingless female in April. These females (the unisexual generation) lay eggs in catkins or on young leaves and produce 'currant galls' in early summer, from which both males and females emerge as the bisexual generation, producing new spangle galls.

Unlike these galls the hard, round 'marble gall' found on twigs on most oaks, has only one unisexual generation, and males have never been found. The female gall wasps emerge in autumn, making a neat hole and laying their eggs in the leaf buds.

The insects hatching from galls are not always those which produced the gall in the first place. Invading insects (*inquilines*) often co-habit, causing no harm to the gall-former and both emerge. Others, however, are parasites either on the gall insect or on the inquilines and use them as food for their own development. These parasitic insects are smaller than their hosts, often minute, and many can grow on one host larva. They too can be featured alongside the gall-formers, so your collection reveals the total story of the plant gall.

5. FARMS AND FOOD

Introduction

History of the British farm

Planning a farm visit

Learning about farm animals

Farm crops

What do I eat?

Where does my food come from?

5. FARMS AND FOOD

Introduction

Much of the British landscape is covered with farmland – green pasture for animal grazing and ploughed fields for growing crops: we still produce a great deal of our own food. It is important that every child knows where his food comes from, so in the following pages we survey the background to British agriculture and take a look at our major food producing livestock and crops. We see how farms can be used educationally and how to plan a farm visit. Finally, we link the farm with the food in the shops and describe some projects that can be done by the town dweller at home.

Farming is the world's largest industry, and a great many people are employed in providing food for others. The farmers in Britain produce over half the nation's food (the rest being imported from other countries). Yet over 70,000 acres of farmland are lost annually to industry, roads and housing: predominantly in south-east England and other highly populated areas, so that the loss is from prime, fertile lowland farmland rather than from the lower grade uplands.

As we travel from one part of this country to another, we pass through a variety of agricultural land. Large fields with few hedgerows characterise the eastern counties, planted with valuable cereal crops of wheat or barley; rich, green pastures are common in the west, where the higher rainfall encourages the growth of grass over long periods of the year and is ideal for dairy and beef cattle; and the hilly and mountainous districts of North Wales, the Pennines, the Lake District and Scotland are often suitable only for sheep farmers. In the flatter drier counties of the south and east, while much of the land is arable (that is, suitable for ploughing for crops), many of the farms are mixed. Here the farmer grows some cereals, and some fodder crops to feed to livestock, and may keep several kinds of animals (cattle, sheep, pigs and poultry) as well. Other farms have developed intensive rearing systems for pigs or poultry, to produce large quantities of meat or eggs in indoor 'batteries', so that the outsider need never realise that animals are there at all.

History of the British Farm

Farming has always been an important part of the British scene and like our woodland owes much of its local character to various European invaders. But its origins can be traced to civilisations far beyond our shores. Cereal crops were grown in the valleys of the Nile, Tigris and Euphrates at least 8000 years ago, and both tools and actual seed stores have been found among archaeological remains. The invention of farming was the most important first step towards 'civilisation', the need for a regular food supply providing the 'necessity towards invention' which led on to yet more development in early times, people worked and lived together, sharing in their toils and success. A settled existence led to greater cultural evolution, since for much of the time people had to wait for crops to grow and lived on stored produce from previous seasons. At about the same time in our history, animals were domesticated, and, except for the dog, reared for food. The earliest herdsman were probably wanderers in nomadic tribes, who traded animals for cereals with the more settled farmers. Later, horses, donkeys and camels were domesticated to provide transport, and oxen introduced to draw the plough.

In some poor and underdeveloped parts of the world many of these simple farming methods can still be seen today. Farming techniques in other parts of the world – in China and South America for instance – may have developed independently of this agricultural revolution in the near East, but it was probably from this centre that they spread to Europe and finally to Britain, arriving in our lands about 5000 years ago.

The first British farmers belonged to the New Stone Age. They brought seeds, sheep and cattle in boats from the Continent, and thus introduced mixed farming in about 3000B.C. Small clearings on hillsides became our first fields, and when soil became poor the farmer moved on to clear new pastures. Much of our early farm history can be told by carbon-dating (that is, by detecting the radio-active content) pollen grains preserved for thousands of years in peat. The acid, wet nature of peat preserves a great number of things, including timber, pottery and pollen. It is possible to take samples of pollen from peat at different depths in the ground – the deeper the deposit the older the pollen grains – and thus to trace the history of our woodlands before and after the Ice Ages, and to discover when wheat and barley were first sown on cleared forest land. Pollen from weeds common in cornfields can be identified in these same peat deposits. Grains of charcoal formed from burned woodlands are also found in the peat, and these too can be dated by their radioactive content to show when man first cleared and burned the native oak woods.

Ancient fields can still themselves be seen on the moors of Devon and Cornwall, and on the downs of Dorset, Wiltshire and nearby counties. In Neolithic times farmers depended more on flocks of sheep and goats, or small herds of cattle or pigs, than on larger areas of crops, and stone enclosures for retaining animals are also still preserved on high desolate moorland such as Bodmin Moor in Cornwall.

About 750BC a type of light plough drawn by two oxen was introduced to Britain by Celtic invaders, and led to the making of fields of more regular rectangular shapes. These Celtic fields are mostly to be seen on light, well-drained soils such as on the chalk South Downs. Deeper storage pits were built as grain stores and villages grew about the farms. With the introduction of iron, the plough became larger and more powerful, so that, drawn by eight oxen, it was capable of clearing large areas of forest for cultivation. Corn grown in southern England was even exported to the Continent, and an important reason for the eventual invasion by the Romans was the fact that Britain was a considerable source of corn.

In later years the Anglo-Saxons introduced further new techniques and once more changed the face of Britain. Large herds of swine were kept in open forests, rooting and browsing on natural fodder such as acorns. A new breed of oxen was introduced to draw ploughs and carts, and sheep grazed almost everywhere, supplying milk for cheese and butter. Each Saxon village was organised to be largely self-supporting, rather than to produce extra quantities of food for trade at home or abroad.

By Norman times the pattern of the Feudal system had settled down, with each village bound to its lord of the Manor and village peasants having regular duties on the land. Already the pattern of traditional English farming was taking shape, and different districts were associated with particular crops or animals. The Cotswolds were famous for excellent wool, Bedfordshire for corn crops and the Vale of the White Horse for dairy and cheese. A great many animals could not be fed in winter, so they were killed and salted. But sheep could still graze when cows ceased to give milk, and ten sheep yielded as much butter and cheese as one cow: only when they ceased to give milk were sheep killed for meat. From the fourteenth century onwards many landowners gave up growing crops and raised sheep instead. Woollen cloth-making became our greatest industry and the wool towns were established. But this created unemployment on the land, since a few shepherds could replace large numbers of agricultural workers, and many of the Tudor villages fell into disrepair and became derelict. The number of sheep continued to increase and each new breed yielded a bigger, heavier fleece.

In the eighteenth century the population was growing and better grain crops were required. The seed drill was invented to hasten planting, and a revolution in British agriculture began. The turnip was introduced to provide winter fodder for cattle, and their winter slaughter became unnecessary. Land growing valuable cereal crops could be rested by planting with turnips, and soil could be improved by planting other crops such as clover. Thus, the Norfolk Four-course rotation, evolved, a system of planting wheat: turnip: barley: clover in each field over a four-year period. Animals were bred by careful selection of stock individuals, specifically for improved meat production.

This was a pioneering period, the origin of modern farming methods. The enclosure of land by Acts of Parliament brought prosperity to big landowners, and more food of better quality to feed an ever-increasing population. Thus, by the early nineteenth century the open fields almost everywhere had been enclosed with hedges and walls: many of our present hedgerows date from that period. But the enclosures also brought ruin to the English peasantry, accustomed to graze their stock on common land, and many of these, as well as farm labourers, emigrated to America and Australia. These people it was who began to develop the great wheatlands, producing vast crops which could later pour back into England. Large areas of our own wheatland consequently ceased to be cultivated. Similarly, with the import of meat products, notably beef and mutton, from these new farmlands, our own meat production rapidly declined.

Dairy farming alone prospered, and it was only the two world wars of this century that forced our historically important farm industry into a new growth phase. Farmers were then urged to plough any waste land, a minimum wage for agriculture was guaranteed and thousands of women worked on the land. Our efficient modern farming methods thus date only from the past forty years, when national farm policies were introduced.

The increased efficiency of British farming has been due to changes both in methods and in crops grown. Old root crops are now replaced by kale, sugar beet, and grass to provide silage. Intensive farming methods have arrived in the eastern counties, demanding larger fields of wheat to enable modern machinery to harvest more rapidly, and carefully selected seed to give increased grain yield. Sheep are reared largely to provide meat and many new breeds have been developed. Dairy stock produce higher yields of milk, and artificial insemination enables the best bulls to pass on particular characteristics to thousands of calves. Intensive rearing of chickens produces cheap eggs and meat, so much so that poultry is no longer a delicacy but features regularly in the British diet. Pigs too can be bred under intensive methods and modern strains yield high quality pork or bacon in short periods. Modern factory farming, irrespective of the controversy it raises, seems here to stay as long as most people require a plentiful meat-based diet at the lowest possible cost.

Planning a farm visit

For many children a visit to a farm can be as exciting as a day spent at the zoo or at the sea. It can also be educationally rewarding, since a great deal can be learned of the ways in which our food is produced. Farms will be accessible according to where you live, but many districts close to large cities have large farms and the City Farms Advisory Service produces a booklet on *Where to find City farms in Britain*. Often such farms are in dense areas of population and provide a unique experience for urban children to see and touch farm animals.

The study you make will depend greatly on the age and ability of the children and on the type of farm you are to visit. However, certain topics are common to most farms and a work sheet can be produced with questions relating to both general and specific features.

First, let's look at the farm buildings. Are they built of local materials? You can make a plan of them and label their uses. Is the haybarn close to the cattle sheds? Where is the manure heap? Are special kinds of buildings and facilities needed for different animals? How many people work on the farm?

What animals are reared on the farm? Is the farm for a specific type of animal or is it mixed? Which breeds are kept and are they especially suited to the locality? Are some animals kept only for 'home use' by the farmer – chickens, a Jersey cow, pigs? Find out details of the way animals are reared (husbandry).

Does the farmer grow any crops? What is the soil like? Are the crops selected for particular soil types? Which crops are grown mainly for cash and which for animal fodder? How large is the farm and how does the farmer use his land? Draw a plan of the fields to show land use. What is an acre? Are the fields large, with few hedges, and ideal for cereal crops or are they small, with good hedges and kept as grassland for grazing? How does the farmer rest his fields (rotation) and how often is each planted with a particular crop? Why is wheat, barley, oats, maize, or other cereal grown in that region? How is silage made?

Farm machinery is greatly enjoyed by children, so perhaps the farmer will demonstrate his tractor and show how he uses it for various jobs on the land. What other machinery does he keep and what does he need to rent from contractors?

Learning about farm animals

You can learn a great deal about farm animals at home or in the classroom. Why not make a farm scrapbook?

Cattle are the most important stock and are kept on most farms. They are able to convert grass, which we cannot eat, into milk: for drinking, and making butter and cheese. Dairy products, like meat, are rich in proteins which we all need for

Fig. 5.1   A dairy cow

growth. Most farmers keep either dairy cows or beef stock, but both need rich pastures on which to graze. Cattle have no upper front teeth and pull out the grass with their muscular tongue, swallowing it whole and allowing initial digestion to occur in the *rumen*, or first stomach. Here bacteria and other micro-organisms start the breakdown of cellulose in the grass and eventually the cow returns this food to the mouth, where she 'chews the cud' with her flat back teeth. The cud when

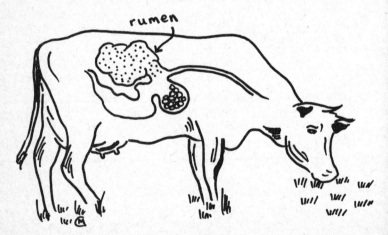

Fig. 5.2   Digestion in a cow

reswallowed enters the second and third stomach chambers, where any undigested food is returned to the rumen, before passing to the fourth stomach for final digestion. It is remarkable that 'grass goes in at one end and milk comes out at the other', and that we owe our thanks to millions of minute bacteria in between! The most common dairy cows are Fresians, which yield a large quantity of milk. Jersey and Guernsey cows, which are of smaller build and have very attractive markings, produce less milk but richer, especially suitable for producing cream. Beef cattle by comparison are much more solid and square in appearance, with fleshy hindquarters, a thick neck and short legs. The Aberdeen Angus and Hereford are common breeds, and are reared from bullocks in remoter districts. Some farms concentrate on breeding cattle, while others, where the quality of pasture is better, produce fat stock. A few cows, such as the Devon, produce both milk and beef and are, therefore, multipurpose.

Sheep live in large flocks and have been bred to suit particular grazing conditions. There are very many different breeds and

Fig. 5.3 Downland sheep

one of the best suited to rich lowland pastures such as the Dorset or Suffolk would not be able to thrive or indeed survive on mountain grassland. Hill sheep like the Black Welsh, Cheviot or Shetland are much hardier, more agile and have coarse long

wool which protects them from a harsh climate. Much of their
time is spent moving about narrow tracks among rocks and
boulders searching for new grazing. Lowland sheep are kept in
fenced fields and have short, thick fleeces. Rams mate in the
autumn with many ewes and each Lowland ewe produces two
or three lambs which fatten quickly, converting the closely-
cropped grass to meat. Hill sheep produce only single lambs,
since much of their food is of poor quality and lambing is often in
early spring when snow lies deep on the ground. Lambs romping
in a field are a sure sign that spring has returned. Pigs are now
most often kept indoors, but small mixed farms still keep a few

Fig. 5.4 Pigs and production

pigs to provide their own pork and bacon. Not long ago most
country people, especially those who were not wealthy, kept a
pig at the bottom of the garden, perhaps among a few apple
trees, fattening it on kitchen scraps and nothing else. Pigs, with a
complete set of teeth closely resembling that of man, are able to
eat just about anything. Many of our early breeds, like the
Gloucester Old Spot, rust-coloured Tamworth and black
Berkshire were popular but produced a fatty pork or bacon.
These primitive breeds, especially the Tamworth, closely re-
semble the native wild boar from which modern pigs have been
bred. They have long snouts for rooting out underground
worms, snails, insects and plant matter; a thicker, hairy coat and

well developed tusks. Wild boars still roam the forests of Europe but are now extinct in England. Even in captivity a pig still roots about, turning over the ground and acting as an efficient plough. After mating with a boar the sow produces in four months a large litter, often 12–14 piglets; she can produce at least two litters each year. The young piglets suckle their mother, as do lambs and calves, but grow more rapidly and can be sold for meat at only four months old, when they may weigh about 120lb. or 'six score' (a score meaning twenty). Today, commercial breeds like the Large White and Landrace are reared intensively, rapidly converting rich manufactured foodstuffs produced from cereal crops into good, lean meat. Due to these new breeds and methods pork is a relatively cheap meat, far cheaper than lamb or beef.

One way to find out more about farm animals is to visit the market in your local town. The market place was a significant feature of early towns and many towns grew to serve the market needs of the neighbouring farming community. The market is always a centre of great activity. Cattle and sheep arrive, to be herded into pens where they are on view to prospective buyers. Auctioneers sell the stock to other farmers, who never appear to be bidding though at the end of the day cattle lorries remove the animals sold to their new farms. Markets are places to buy your other farm needs too – foodstuffs, hay, tools, clothing and machinery. Farmers are able to meet other farmers to discuss their problems, speak to the local vet and representatives of agricultural companies.

Farm crops

Look at the fields around your home or school, or along the road or railway when you go on a journey, and make a list of which plant crops are grown in a particular area. Plants are an essential feature of most farms, since even the dairy or beef farmer probably grows some grass to make hay and root crops as winter feed. The most important crops of the arable farmer are cereals or grain crops. Barley is most popular since it ripens quickly, and can be grown from the south into the far north of Scotland. It is used for beer and feeding livestock. Wheat is an important grain crop in eastern England, and produces a valuable crop for bread, biscuits and breakfast cereals. Both

Fig. 5.5 Cereal crops: a. wheat   b. maize   c. barley   d. oats   e. rye

wheat and barley are sown in the autumn, and in spring the young plants are dressed with fertiliser and the soil is broken by harrowing, and then rolled. The rolling may crush some small plants but will encourage each to produce several shoots or tillers, each capable of making an ear of corn. Oats and rye are now scarce in England but some farms in Scotland still grow the traditional breakfast porridge oat crop.

Harvest time is a busy one on the farm. Timing the operation is critical for the crop must be cut and stored in dry weather. Modern combine harvesters can cut and thresh as much as ten tons of grain an hour. The straw is thrown out and either ploughed back into the earth to form humus and improve soil structure, or baled for use by livestock. Grain is stored in immense, tall, metal silos, each with a perforated floor through which hot air can be blown to dry the seed thoroughly. The grain silo has become a new feature of the British farm landscape.

Hay is usually harvested in June or July, earlier in the south than the north. It will provide winter food for cattle and other animals when fresh grass is no longer available. It must be cut and harvested while dry, and with modern methods may be ready in two days for the baler. The once familiar haystack or 'rick' is now replaced by a Dutch barn (an open, roofed structure) in which the hay can be stored dry. Different varieties of grass yield different types of hay, and some will grow better under particular soil and climatic conditions than others. Fertilisers containing nitrates and phosphates give increased yields of grass, and manure from the livestock is often scattered on to the fields by a mechanical spreader.

Some farmers cut grass while it is still green and rich in food value and pack it tightly into a silo tower or pit. When the silo is full it is covered with earth and straw and the grass keeps fresh and moist until winter, when it is fed to cattle as silage.

These forage crops enrich the soil by their association with bacteria contained in small nodules on their roots. The microbes are able to use nitrogen in the environment and convert it into nitrates (*nitrogen fixation*) which can be absorbed by the plant and assist growth. After harvesting the green crop the roots, and their nodules, are ploughed back into the soil, thus improving its nutrient quality and structure.

The most frequently grown root crop is the potato, which still forms an important part of our diet, supplying carbohydrate for energy production. Different varieties yield crops from February until autumn, and although early potatoes are best suited to light, sandy soils the main crop can be grown on much heavier soils. Small, well-selected potatoes are planted in furrows in the spring to yield the main crop, and modern machinery is available both for planting and harvesting. Traditionally, storage was in a 'clamp'; the potatoes were piled on to a flat piece of ground in a heap a few feet high and then covered with straw and earth to keep out frost and the light. Today however potatoes tend simply to be kept in well insulated buildings.

Root crops are often planted after a field has produced wheat, since it cleans the field of weeds due to ploughing, ridging and harvesting, and does not take such a high level of nutrients from the soil. Some root crops, such as turnips, swedes and mangelwurzels, are cultivated at a similar time in the rotation to supply winter animal feed for cattle and sheep. In Norfolk and other parts of East Anglia the most common root crop is sugar beet, which yields a cash-crop for sugar extraction. The dried pulp which remains can then be used as animal fodder and the green beet tops are fed fresh to livestock. Nearly a third of our sugar needs are supplied by home-grown beet.

What do I eat?

A good project to start at home is to make a chart of what you eat each day. Make a full list of each type of food, separating foodstuffs into groups – drinks, vegetables, cereals, fruit, meat, dairy products and so forth. Draw seven columns, one for each day, beside your food list and mark each time you eat a particular product. At the end of the week see what foods are most often encountered in your diet. What makes up most of the bulk? Can you calculate how much milk you drink each week? A dairy cow produces an average nine litres per day, so how many people will that supply each week? Which of your foods come from plants and which from animals? Place 'P' or 'A' against each food in your list. Are your 'bulk foods' derived from plants or animals? Foods must supply the essential carbohydrates, fats and proteins you need for growth and energy, but other items must be present in your diet for healthy body function, especially vitamins. Some of these are supplied by plants and others by animals. Fruit and vegetables are rich in vitamin C and cereals provide vitamin B. Milk, dairy products and eggs contain vitamin A and animal fats and oils are rich sources of vitamin D. You can learn a great deal about your body and its functioning by examining what you eat.

Where does my food come from?

We have already undertaken a shopping survey, and seen how food is sold in the supermarket. Fresh potatoes come in polythene bags, but chips are solid white sticks surrounded by ice, and crisps come in little packets. Peas are sold frozen or in tins. Chickens are plucked of their feathers, frozen and polythene wrapped. None of these much resembles the plants and animals on the farm.

So where does it come from? Some of your foods are certainly produced on land near your home, but many come from far-away places, with a very different climate from our own. It is interesting and easy to find out about the products of other countries by visiting your local supermarket and examining the food in the cupboard at home.

You might begin by tracing from an atlas an outline map of the world, showing the main countries. Fix this in the centre of a large sheet of paper, such as an old length of wallpaper, and then collect labels from food tins and packets. Stick them around the map with arrows indicating the country where each was produced. Different colours can indicate the major food-producing areas: beef, dairy produce, lamb, fruit, cereals, coffee, tea, sugar . . . until finally you can see how the food we eat arrives from every corner of the world.

Find out which parts of plants produce different foods and how they are used to make the things you eat. What is your favourite packed lunch for school? A chocolate wafer biscuit, crisps and orange juice, a banana? Each is made from plants from many parts of the world. Chocolate is made from cocoa beans grown in West Africa and the West Indies. The beans are really the seeds of the cocoa tree, found in large pods among the branches. The beans are roasted and ground into a fine powder from which bars of chocolate can be made in a factory. The wafer biscuit is made from wheat grains, grown at home or in the vast wheat fields of Canada or America, and milled into flour for baking. Crisps of course are made from potatoes – which are really the swollen underground stems of the plant. The potatoes are cleaned, sliced finely and cooked in hot oil until crisp and golden. The oil may have been vegetable in origin, produced from maize (corn) seeds grown in America, but many oils are derived from animal fats. Bananas grow in bunches on large palms in the West Indian islands of Jamaica and Trinidad. They are cut down by local plantation workers and sent here in cargo ships. Oranges grow on trees in Spain and other countries around the Mediterranean. Their crushed fruit is sweetened with sugar – in turn made from sugar cane grown in the West Indies or South America, or sugar beet from East Anglia – and made into orange juice. Sugar cane is the stem of tall, woody grass-like plants, while sugar beet is a swollen root of the plant. And so each of our favourite foods has its own story to tell. Next time you go shopping think about some others, and add them to your chart.

6. WATER

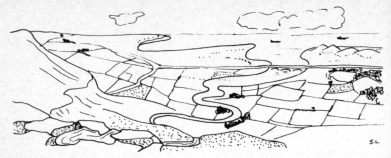

Introduction

Water and life

Rain

The changing face of the river

Making a river study

River nature trails

Ponds

Pond life – living together

Newts, frogs and toads – the amphibians

Keeping an aquarium

Lakes and reservoirs

Seasons of the lake

Lakes and man

Canals

Coarse fishing

6. WATER

Introduction

Water is essential for life. It is also a fascinating study and a compulsive medium for play, for children and adults. And there is water everywhere: in the open countryside, in the city and the town. Canals, rivers, ponds and lakes are often to be found even in a large city centre, and access is not necessarily difficult for wheelchair users. You can also learn a great deal at home with only an aquarium or a jar of tadpoles!

In this chapter we examine a variety of freshwater environments, looking at their geography and natural history. We see how rain is formed and contributes to the origin of streams. After following the stream to the river mouth we learn how to study a river and use the riverbank as a nature trail. Pond life demonstrates well the close inter-relationships of plants and animals, food chains and production; we shall list things to look for. We shall describe the problems – and fun – of the home aquarium, and suggest projects. Wildlife of lakes and reservoirs can be highly rewarding to watch, and a canal holiday might be within reach of handicapped people. Finally, we look at fishing as a recreational activity for disabled people, and learn a little about how to go about becoming an angler.

Water and life

Much of our food, whether obtained from plants or animals, is largely water. Salad vegetables contain as much as 95 per cent, fruit about 80 per cent and meat 65 per cent water. Even our own bodies have considerable water content, about 55–65 per cent, but in that of some soft bodied animals, such as worms and jellyfish, it may well be nearly the whole of their body weight! Water is essential for life. Green plants absorb water through their roots and convert it, together with carbon dioxide in the air, into foods such as sugar and starch. This process, which

requires the energy of sunlight, is known as *photosynthesis* and is
the basis of all food production.

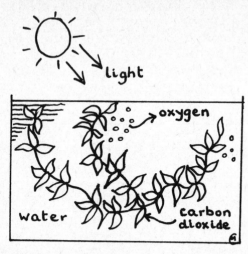

Fig. 6.1 How plants make food

More water than is required for photosynthesis enters the
plant, since it is only in this manner that essential mineral
nutrients can be absorbed from the soil and transported through
the plant. Water and its dissolved nutrients pass from the roots,
into the stem and then into the veins of the leaves. But that water
must then leave the plant. If you cover a plant in a pot with a
large jar or polythene bag, you will notice that after a few hours
the inside of the bag becomes damp and eventually wet. Water
has left the plant via small pores (or *stomata*) on the leaf surface, a
process called *transpiration*. In tall trees, this 'transpiration
stream' of water passing through the plant is able to carry raw
materials to great heights, and in the course of its passage
through the plant the water has also provided much of the
support it needs to stand upright – a feature especially
important in non-woody plants. Plants living in arid conditions,
such as sand dunes and deserts, evolve mechanisms to reduce
their water loss. Cacti reduce their leaf surface by forming
spines, and evolve a waxy outer covering of the fleshy stems.
Special cells inside are capable of storing water. Marram grass
on coastal dunes has narrow, rolled leaves, with the stomata

sunk into grooves on the inner surface, and surrounded by hairs. Water uptake in these *xerophytic* plants is greatly enhanced by long underground stems and root systems, which tap water from a wide area.

Man too requires great quantities of water, an adult taking in and losing about five pints ($2\frac{1}{2}$ litres) each day. This amount obviously increases under hot conditions, or when a great deal of exercise and work is being done. Much of this water is needed simply to cool the body – by sweating – and thus maintaining a constant internal temperature. Sweating however applies only to mammals. Birds too need a constant temperature, but they cannot sweat because of the presence of their feathers. Instead they lose heat by evaporating water as they breathe.

Water is needed by all animals to remove waste excretory products before they poison the body. Mammals produce urine, which is largely water containing the substance *urea*. We excrete just under three pints each day ($1\frac{1}{2}$ litres), the remainder of our water being lost via the skin and expired air from the lungs. For some animals however this degree of water loss would mean death, and they have special adaptations to reduce loss. Desert animals, such as reptiles and insects, avoid the heat of the day by hiding in shady conditions, under stones and scrub or in holes in the sand. They are active at night when it is cool and they need not sweat. They excrete a dry, white powder (*uric acid*) which needs no water for its removal from the body. Some desert rodents, like the kangaroo rat, remove waste products in a small volume of very concentrated urine and can survive on the water in their dry food, together with the water manufactured in the body as a by-product of energy release. Camels, contrary to popular belief, do not store water but conserve carefully what they take in with their food. But where does our water come from?

Rain

Most water is contained in the vast oceans which cover about three-quarters of the world. But sea water contains large quantities of dissolved salts, making it saline. If you take a litre of sea water and allow it to evaporate out completely it leaves behind about 35 grammes of salts, mostly sodium chloride – table salt. The salinity of seawater is thus 35 parts per thousand

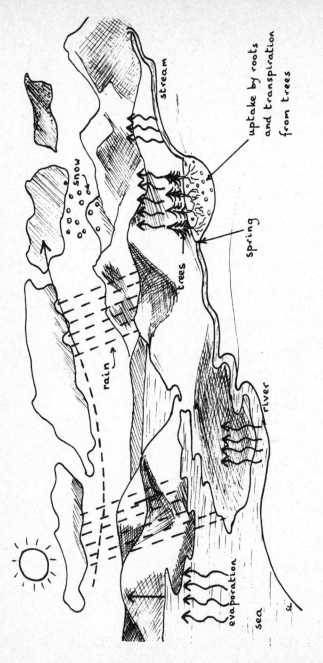

Fig. 6.2 The water cycle

and does not vary greatly, except in a few inland seas such as the Dead Sea. Plants and animals however require 'fresh' and not 'salt' water.

Our rain begins its life in the sea. Surface waters of the ocean are constantly evaporating, especially under hot conditions, and the water vapour rises to form clouds in the sky. As they float higher so the water vapour cools and condenses as water droplets, which may stay in the clouds for a long time. With on-shore winds clouds drift across the land, rising higher about hills and mountains, and with greater cooling in the high atmosphere the water droplets become too heavy for the cloud to carry and they fall – as rain. Some water vapour in the air also condenses on the colder ground surface at night to form water droplets that we recognise as dew. Dew is very important in deserts and on dunes, and is a major source of water in these environments.

Often the water droplets become so cold they turn into ice pellets in the clouds and fall to the ground as snow in cold weather. Those that melt as they approach the ground may turn to sleet or very cold rain. Sometimes ice pellets in the clouds grow in size as more water vapour freezes on them, and form large hail stones. If you could look inside a hailstone it would be seen to consist of concentric bands of different thicknesses.

Rain or snow supply the streams and rivers with all their water. It may enter directly on the surface of the land or drain into the soil between rocks and become underground water. This is especially true in limestone and chalk areas, where the rock is soft and permeable and water penetrates via cracks or faults in the rock. This water may flow many miles beneath the ground, cutting out caves during its passage, but eventually it will meet an impermeable rock layer and be forced to the surface as a spring. Many large rivers (the Severn and Fowey for instance) begin life as a spring or collection of springs. Streams and rivers eventually pass to the sea, fresh water meeting seawater at the estuary and thus the water cycle is completed.

The changing face of the river

Most rivers have their source in the high mountains and moorlands – Dartmoor, the Pennines, Snowdonia, and the Scottish Highlands. Here, rainfall is higher and surface waters meet to form downward, rushing torrents tumbling over rocks to

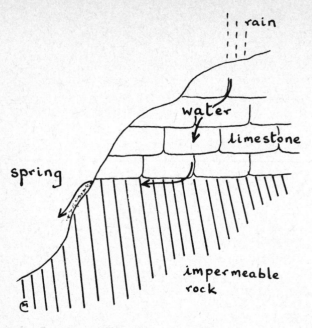

Fig. 6.3 Underground water

form small falls and provide a major force or erosion. Rocks become worn by the continuous passage of water carrying rock debris until finally a gorge or steep-sided valley may form, especially where the rock is soft. Small particles of rock are carried rapidly onward and only large boulders and stones remain to form the stream bed. Few plants can grow here, but often the rocks are covered by a green moss carpet (*Fontinalis*) or by a slimy growth of algae. Animals must seek shelter beneath stones or be washed away. The small fresh-water limpet clings close to the rock by a muscular foot. The young stages or nymphs of mayflies and stoneflies press close against the stone, merging in colour with the green-brown background of rock and slime. Larvae of blackflies (*Simulium*) have strong hooks at the rear end for attachment and many caddis fly larvae form protective cases of small rock particles which they spin together and attach to the stone surface. Finding animal life in rapid streams can mean turning over countless rocks for very little return: many that you examine will bear no apparent life. But as you follow the 'head stream' downhill it broadens out into a 'trout beck', slowing in pace and gaining a richer fauna. The

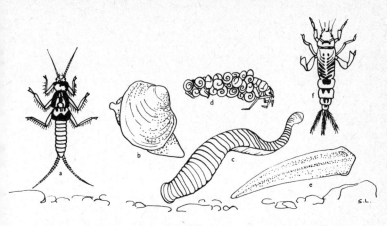

Fig. 6.4   Animals of the stream: a. stonefly nymph   b. freshwater limpet   c. horse leech   d. caddis larva   e. flat worm   f. mayfly nymph

stream becomes wider and shallower and the gravel bottom permits anchorage for the roots of some water plants. Water crowfoot, white flowers opening at the water surface in summer, has narrow, strap-like leaves which give little resistance to the flow of water. Some species of pond-weed (*Potamogeton*) have broader, flat leaves which float on the surface and may provide cover for water snails. There is a greater variety of insect life and caddis, and stoneflies and mayflies will be joined by the young stages of dragonflies and damselflies. Leeches cling to the stones and water plants, looping along with suckers at each end. Small flatworms (*Planaria*), black or cream in colour, creep across a stone surface, and freshwater shrimps (*Gammarus*) lurk in cracks in stones or within the gravel bed. The animals of the beck provide food for water birds like the dipper, which is able to swim underwater and feed on caddis fly larvae. Often the dipper is seen bobbing up and down while perched on a stone surrounded by moving water. Grey wagtails search the banks for insects which have hatched from their aquatic larvae and nymphs, and in summer swallows and martins fly above the water feeding on black-flies, midges and mosquitoes. A king-

fisher, irridescent blue and bright salmon-pink, darts un-
observed along the bank or sits in wait on a branch. Small fish
are its prey and are skilfully caught in the long, pointed beak.
Few fish dwell in the very fast flowing waters of the hillside beck,
but trout love these conditions, rich in insect food and oxygen
from the tumbling waters. It is to this region of the river that the
'brown' trout moves in winter to spawn. The longer migrations
of the 'sea' trout are more dramatic, though both are in fact the
same species. The salmon too migrates vast distances, from the
mid-Atlantic Ocean to the upper stretches of the river where
spawning occurs. The adult fish changes in structure and
physiology during this movement from a saline to freshwater

Fig. 6.5   Salmon leaping

environment. It must fight against the flow of water and jump
high over waterfalls and weirs – the famous salmon leaps. The
female lays her eggs in a scrape in the river bed, the male sheds
sperm over thcm, and after fertilisation they are covered by the
parents until hatching. After spawning, the adults may die. But
some make the return journey to the sea, and the following year
repeat the same migration. Young salmon stay for two or three
years in their freshwater haunts, gradually drifting down
towards the estuary and their marine feeding grounds. After a
further two or three years in the sea they return to their ancestral

home in the rivers of mountains and moors.

Other fish inhabit the upper reaches of the river. The Miller's Thumb or Bullhead adapts to the colour of its background most perfectly, and the Grayling is a schooling fish which breeds in the submountain regions of the river.

Eventually the hills are left behind, and as the river gets slower mud settles. More plants grow and the banks are colonised by willows and alders. This is the 'minnow reach' named after a commonly encountered fish of this region. The minnow is a small fish up to 10 centimetres (three inches) long, which in the breeding season of spring and early summer produces vivid colours in the male. The bases of his paired fins and tail fin become bright red, stimulating the females to lay eggs. The male stickleback similarly develops a bright red colouration on the undersurface. He builds a nest from bits of vegetation into which he drives the female and where she spawns. The male guards the nest with the eggs, and later the fish fry. The stickleback of freshwaters has three spines along the

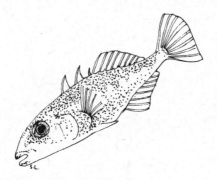

Fig. 6.6 The three-spined stickleback

centre of the back, and although found in this part of the river will also inhabit slower flowing regions, ponds and lakes. Trees growing along the banks encourage more birdlife, and in spring small willow warblers and chiffchaffs from Africa return and sing from the leafy canopy alongside marsh and willow tits.

When the river reaches the flat land it flows very slowly, and the curves of the river channel develop into broad loops or *meanders*. The river plain from above is seen as a flat fertile landscape with the twisting river gradually widening as it nears the sea. Where meanders touch on opposite banks small curved narrow *ox-bow lakes* become isolated at the side of the river. This

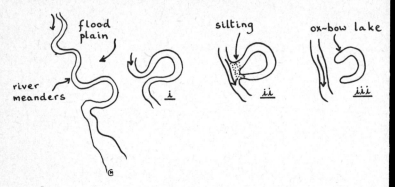

Fig. 6.7   Formation of an ox-bowlake

stretch of the river easily floods after heavy rain and when tides are high, spreading a layer of fine river sediment or silt over the flood plain and adding to its fertility. This sluggish lowland reach has a rich muddy bottom, as the water force is too slow to carry even the smallest materials. The water is rich in nutrients and dense growths of plants colonise the river margin. Flag iris produce bright yellow flowers in early summer; the great reed mace, often wrongly called the bulrush, is commonly recognised by the dense brown seedhead and tall, pointed leaves; the bur-reed has round, spiky fruits and long, flat leaves; the water plantain has tall spikes of white or pink flowers and very broad oval leaves. On the wet banks yellow clumps of marsh marigold or kingcup flower under a willow tree and the tall white meadow sweet presents a fragrant scent in mid-summer. In the open water yellow or white lilies float on the surface – large, round, single flowers settled among a mass of large floating leaves. Pondweeds, arrowhead and mare's tail appear above the water surface, all plants adapted to life in a water environment. Moorhen, coot and water rail skulk among the reeds and other vegetation; a heron waits silently for an unsuspecting fish or frog; and a dabchick plunges down below the surface waters in search of food. Mammals too may burrow along the river banks.

Water voles leave their hole just above the water level, swimming strongly across the river. An otter leaves the water with a fine, silvery fish, while in some districts the mink is a familiar sight along a river bank, where escapees from fur farms have established a colony. Fish too are more frequent in this stretch, hiding among dense plant growth and feeding on a wealth of insect life. Perch, roach and pike are commonly taken by the angler.

Finally the river meets the sea, a region of differing environments. Neither freshwater nor marine – a region peculiar to itself. As the tide retreats salt marshes remain, home ·of the wading bird and salt-tolerant plant. The estuarine reach of the river represents the end of the journey of perhaps several hundred miles from the high lands of the mountain to the flat lands at sea-level.

Making a river study

This is an ideal project for a day's journey in the car, although to give the study the time it deserves will also involve several visits to each stretch of the river. First trace your river to its source on the O.S. map and make a sketch map showing where it begins and ends, and the countryside and places it passes on route to the sea. Mark any bridges and points where a road meets the river, since these will be your points of investigation by car. It may not be possible to take a wheelchair all the way to the source, high in a hilly district, but since many streams in that district will be similar, a more accessible one can be used as a starting point. In the field, try to find out more about each stretch of the river. The bottom material can be sampled, brought home in a tin and dried out, then passed through sieves to show size of rock material. Is the bottom formed mainly of rocks, stones, gravel, sand or mud?

Bring home a sample of water in a large polythene bottle, add a few drops of washing-up liquid and see if you can easily make a good foam. How many drops must you add? Try washing your hands in this water. Streams as they pass over the rocks collect minerals. In districts where rocks, such as granite, are hard the water collects few minerals and is called soft, easily making a good foam with soap. Hard waters are found in limestone and chalk districts (the Cotswolds, Chilterns, Mendips), since a great deal of 'lime' is dissolved in it. Such water forms scum with soap and is 'hard' to wash with. Hard waters form *stalagmites* (grow up) and *stalactites* (grow down) in caves in such areas.

Measure the width of the stream or river, and water depth, with the aid of a tape or marked stick, which you can make beforehand. In order to find out how fast the water flows take a few corks, pieces of polythene waste or the sticks from ice lollies. Measure a known distance, say 10 metres, along the river and while you stay at the beginning ask your friend to wait at the end. Drop your 'float' into the water and record the time it takes (in seconds) to flow along the stretch. Repeat at least three times (some may become stuck on a rock or in vegetation) and average your results. This is a modification of 'Pooh sticks', a popular game often played from a bridge over a river. The rate of flow is distance divided by time (e.g. stream 2m./sec.; river 30cm./sec.

Finally, make a full collection of plants and animals at each site on your river. Look under stones, pieces of wood, in vegetation and use a net in more open stretches. Examine your small animals with a lens and identify each, as well as possible, with a good book. Make a list for each stretch of river, indicating where you found the particular species. Animals can be examined in a white polythene washing-up bowl, with smaller containers such as plastic margarine pots to hold individuals. Excess water can be drained away through a plastic tea strainer, leaving the small insects and crustacea behind in the sieve. Use a fine paint brush to pick up very small and delicate animals, and transfer them to a small quantity of water in a dish. It is not too difficult to find out the major groups of fresh-water invertebrate life.

Remember to replace all stones as you find them – do not leave them on the banks of the stream. They are the homes of many small creatures and without them they will not survive.

River nature trails

Just as it is possible to design a nature trail on a reserve, in a woodland or in a town centre, so it is possible to think of the waterside as a good place to walk with handicapped people. I introduced a very severely physically and mentally handicapped girl, from a sub-normality hospital unit, to the pleasures of an outdoor life this way. Her wheelchair was in fact a 'stretcher on wheels', but we found a stretch where the access was good and the path surface reasonable. Many rivers flow through town parks and allow for public recreation. So the walk need not be long and arduous for it to be enjoyable and stimulating. Indeed, it is often best to think simple! Find a short length of river or canal close to the town centre and everything else follows from there. Trees, flowers, birds, insects all flourish along a short stretch of waterside. The fact that you are out of doors may be sufficient, but it is not too difficult to improve the quality of the walk by finding out more about the wildlife living there.

What is the name of the river; where does it flow from and to? If your waterside is a canal, what is its name and when was it built? What were the main uses? Is it used for fishing? What fish are caught? Look at the trees, especially in summer and autumn, growing along the banks. Identify them from leaves and fruits. Willow, alder, poplar, ash are often encountered. Look for patches of flowers which may be typical of waterside habitats; the tall Himalayan Balsam with large pink-purple flowers common in July; the yellow flag, looking like garden iris, growing with roots in the shallow water and flowering in May; and red water avens with fruits covered in long spines ('burrs'). Riverside plants are easy to spot in a book with colour illustrations, of which many are available.

Trees and plants stay in the same place over a period of time, and you can plan your walk or repeat it on several occasions. Animals unfortunately run, fly, and jump and will not be where you last saw them. However, ducks, swans, coot and moorhen tend always to be around somewhere, if you know where they like to live. Keep your eyes open and point out anything you see. A diary of your walk will make interesting reading in later months or years, and you will be surprised at just how much there is to see along a single stretch of water.

Ponds
Ponding is fun! I know of nothing better to excite a child, or for that matter Mum and Dad, than dipping a net into a pond and emptying the contents into a white plastic bowl. Everyone immediately wants to have their dip – 'please can we have the net?' – and then crowds around to examine the contents. Even a small pond can support a surprising variety of life whether it is in

wild, open countryside or in a depression on the local waste ground. Most children at some time in their lives have returned home, proud faced, with a jar held by a string handle and containing the precious collection of 'taddies'. There is an annual springtime influx of tadpoles into all primary school classrooms for the nature table. Handicapped youngsters too should experience these delights, and know what it is like to feel water flowing over the tops of Wellington boots! Wheelchairs can be set alongside the pond. We take most of our wheelchairs, and their users, out into our pond, which is fortunately shallow and has a hard bed, so that they can really feel part of that environment.

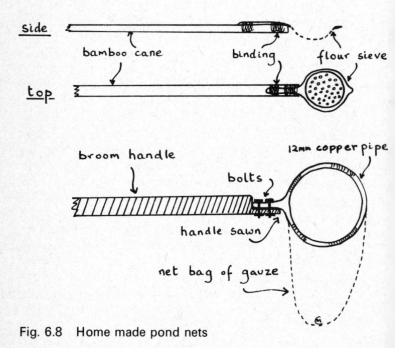

Fig. 6.8   Home made pond nets

Pond nets may be purchased or made at home from a strong bamboo cane, to which you attach a plastic flour sieve, tightly binding the handle to the cane with string. This has the added advantage of being very light to use for those with poor hand control or neuro-muscular handicap. Alternatively, the net frame can be made from good stiff galvanised wire bent into a circle or triangle: a triangle is best since it gives a straight edge to push along the bottom of the pond. Make the net bag with some material which allows water to pass through a fine mesh, thus retaining the small animals and water plants: muslin, nylon gauze or a wine-straining bag from one of the larger chemists shops are all suitable.

Pond life – living together

The pond is a well defined community of animals and plants, living together in a balanced system. Food for the community is provided partially by the plants themselves, through their photosynthesis, and partially by detritus supplied mainly as leaves from nearby trees. If the pond is too heavily covered with leaves each year however it will not be able to cope, since the bacteria which decompose this detritus use a great deal of oxygen, leaving the pond deficient of this essential gas. Other organisms, especially fish, will not be able to breathe and gradually the pond will become stagnant and smelly. Such ponds are unlikely to survive in nature and most that you visit will be open and airy, rich in animal life.

Some animals feed directly on the numerous kinds of pondweed – they are called 'herbivores'; others feed on the bottom detritus and are called 'scavengers'. Animals eat other animals and are the 'carnivores' of the community. There are various levels of carnivores in the system, ultimately ending with the few large predatory animals living in or near the pond. Fish, such as the pike, and birds like the heron represent the ends of their food chains. If we trace the many food chains in the pond and seek the numerous feeding links between plants and various animals, we find that there is an intricate web of inter-relationships rather than a series of individual chains.

It is important that all parts of the pond are utilised for living and feeding, to avoid competition between species. Thus, we find that the water surface is colonised by the floating leaves of duckweed or the filament strands of the alga called *Spirogyra*, which often gives the appearance of green slime. Surface insects such as pond skaters slide rapidly across the water, held in position by surface tension of the water film. Whirligig beetles spin about, aggregating in patches of bright sunlight, in search

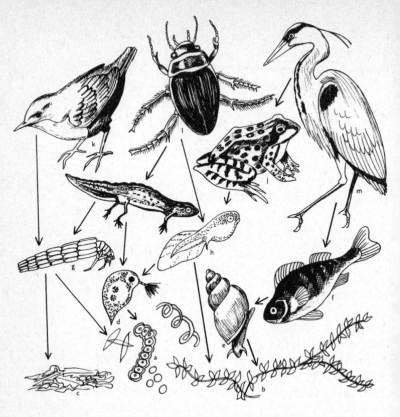

Fig. 6.9   A pond food web: a. algae   b. pondweed   c. detritus   d. water flea   e. pond snail   f. perch   g. caddis larvae   h. tadpole   i. newt   j. frog   k. dipper   l. diving beetle   m. heron

of food. The water scorpion lives in the shallow water at the pond edge; dark and well camouflaged against the background of rotting leaves, he uses a long breathing tube at the rear end to obtain air from above the water surface. Other insects swim freely about the pond. Water boatmen, of several types, have long back legs fringed with hairs which function as oars, rowing these detritus-feeders from the bottom to the surface. Members of one large species, often called 'backswimmers' because of their habit of swimming upside down, are predatory, piercing their insect prey with fine needle-like mouth parts and sucking out the body juices. They give you quite a sharp stinging sensation in the fingers when you pick them up!

There are numerous water beetles in the pond, swimming strongly and trapping air at the surface of the water, which they take down into the depths as a small air bubble. This may give them a silvery appearance. Eventually the air supply is exhausted and they must return to the surface for a new supply. The largest and most dramatic is the Great Diving Beetle, over an inch long and very robust.

Many pond insects, like those we found in the stream, are really larvae and nymphs of insects which spend their adult life flying above the pond. Dragonflies and damselflies have bright metallic colours – red, blue, green. Their wings are large and have fine veins supporting them, so they fly strongly. They are capable of leaving the pond behind and moving into woods, fields and moors. But it is to water that they must return to lay eggs and for the development of their young nymphal stages. Ponding in the spring and summer produces many such juvenile insects, mostly looking very unlike their future adult stages. Who would think the squat, brown, ugly nymph would emerge ultimately as a beautiful brightly coloured dragonfly? Mayflies, stoneflies, alderflies and caddis flies all develop in this manner. Some feed on detritus, others on smaller animal life, but together they make the pond community a well balanced living world.

Newts, frogs and toads – the amphibians

Frogspawn is still a common sight in early spring, although due to drainage of land for building and farming the frog has fewer places to lay her eggs today than in former years. Any expanse of water, from small farm puddles and roadside ditches to large lakes and reservoirs, will serve as a breeding ground. At the time of spawning frogs assemble in large numbers, often of more than a thousand, croaking at night and providing good food supply for larger predators. The smaller male mates with many females, and as each female sheds her eggs into the water they are fertilised by the male. Development of the egg, surrounded by its protective jelly-envelope, takes about three months to produce a new baby frog. The young tadpoles hatch in between one and

Fig. 6.10 The world of the pond: a. dragonfly b. swallow c. water plantain d. moorhen e. pond skater f. water lily g. water boatman h. water scorpion i. Canadian pondweed j. mayfly k. common reed l. heron m. reedmace n. coot o. great diving beetle p. broad leaved pondweed q. mallard r. stonewort s. watervole

two weeks, depending on the temperature, and feed initially on water plants. They have gills on the throat region to breath the oxygen dissolved in the water, but later these external gills disappear and are replaced by internal gills similar to those of the fish. Small back legs soon appear and are later joined by the front legs. During this period the tadpole must eat animal matter in order to complete a successful development. Eventu-

ally, as the tadpole nears the end of its larval life, the gills are
replaced by lungs, the legs are fully formed and the tail shrinks
to a tiny stub. The young frog, only 1cm long, is ready to leave
the pond, but it will not be fully grown for another three years.
This transition from tadpole to adult is called *metamorphosis*, and
is a pattern of development similar to that seen in the life history
of a butterfly or moth.

   Although frog spawn may contain several thousand small
black eggs, only a few young frogs survive. Tadpoles are eaten
by predatory insects and the small frogs are easy prey to
waterside birds. Even larger frogs form the main diet for herons.
The adult frog can live away from water but must be kept moist
in damp vegetation or mud. Toads by comparison can live in
drier environments, especially towns. They have a thicker,

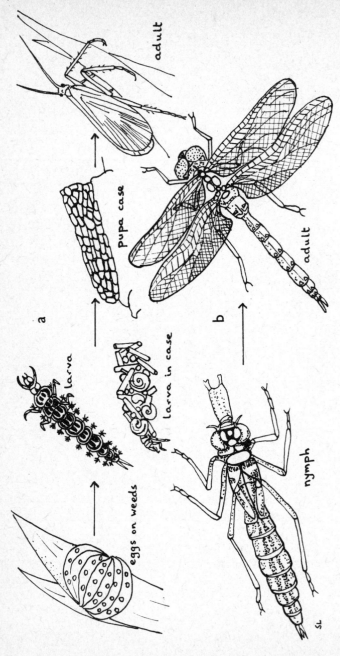

Fig. 6.11   Insect life histories: a. caddis fly   b. dragonfly

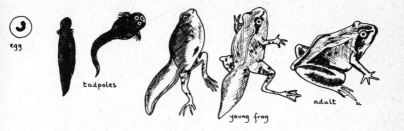

Fig. 6.12   Life history of the frog

Fig. 6.13   Life history of the newt

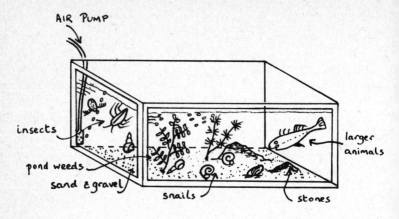

Fig. 6.14   Keeping an aquarium

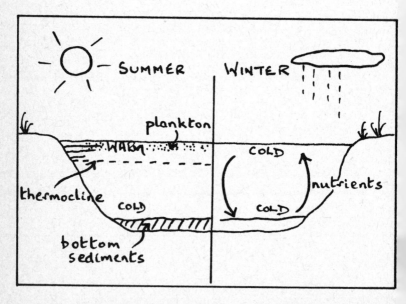

Fig. 6.15   Seasons of the lake

warty skin and do not desiccate so easily. Unlike frogs they survive attacks by predators, since they taste bitter and are spat-out when taken by dogs and other mammals. Toads can also puff themselves into a large bloated shape which makes them difficult to eat and frightens away potential enemies. But like frogs it is to water they they must return for breeding. The spawn of a toad is ribbon-like, each string of black eggs surrounded in jelly and reaching several feet in length.

A more attractive amphibian is the newt. In England there are three species to be encountered: the smooth, palmate and crested newts. In the breeding season male newts are brightly coloured and may have a large crest along their back. Like their relatives they produce tadpoles with external gills, but the eggs are laid singly on water plants. The adult newt retains its tail after metamorphosis and closely resembles the younger newt stages. Often adults stay in the pond even during winter, but they can leave the water and spend their time in damp vegetation close to their breeding place.

You can observe the development of the frog through all its stages in school or at home. Collect a small piece of spawn and keep it in pond water in a large sweet jar. (Too many young tadpoles will compete for food and air and eventually die.) As the time approaches when the tadpoles are due to complete development they should be transferred to an aquarium, or at least to a container with large surface area in which some large stones can be placed above the water level. This allows young frogs to leave the water and use their lungs. Give young tadpoles water plants as food, but as they grow hang small pieces of fresh raw meat in the tank, and change these every few days.

The new frogs should be returned to the same pond as you found the spawn. Keep adult frogs, toads and newts for short periods in a vivarium. This can be a large polythene box, kept damp but not full of water. Soil, moss and plants are suitable materials to place in the box, with stones and rotting wood to give shelter. Feed them on worms and insects such as small flies. Provide a small 'pond' in your vivarium by filling a shallow bowl or saucer with water. Never place an aquarium or vivarium in a bright sunny place and remember to check your animals every day to remove dead and decaying material quickly.

Keeping an aquarium

You will be able to keep your own pond in the kitchen, living room or bedroom if you decide to establish an aquarium. Pond life is relatively easy to keep alive, provided you observe one or two rules. The aquarium can be purchased in a local pet shop and should measure about 60cm long × 30cm wide and 30cm deep. Most now have plastic-covered frames, but some still have a frame of painted metal. If you are unable to obtain such a tank, a rectangular plastic bread-bin or cake container would be suitable, but clear plastic is best since then you can look through the sides, rather than merely from above. Place a 2–3 cm layer of clean gravel or sand at the bottom of your tank, and fill slowly with pond water or rain water. If you use tap water allow the tank to stand for a few days before introducing pond animals since domestic water is treated with chlorine for purification. A piece of brown parcel paper on top of the gravel bed will stop the water stirring up sand and fine material, thus clouding the water. Run the water on to the paper and then gently remove the paper once the tank is full. Add water plants, from the pond, planting their roots in the gravel and sand; some plants float free in the water. The most popular is Canadian pondweed, which produces oxygen especially in good sunlight, to be used by the water animals for breathing. Water Milfoil and Broad-leaved pondweed are also suitable. Do not over-plant since leaves fall and decay and can stagnate the tank. Add some pond snails to graze on the minute green algae (slime), which can soon cover the inside of the tank walls if you place the tank in too much light. A few stones at the bottom will provide shelter for some small animals, but be careful not to add the really ferocious predators such as Great Diving Beetle, 'Back-swimmer' and Water Scorpion since they will soon eat everything else. A stickleback, minnow or stoneloach adds great interest. Newts too will enhance your tank, but remember to provide some means of them leaving the water. The pond is a delicately balanced community of plants and animals. Your tank should likewise not be over-stocked. A few live animals are better than a lot of dead ones!

Lakes and reservoirs

Lakes are formed in several ways: some by the action of ice, as in mountain areas such as Scotland; others, in lowland districts, by sinking of land; and some by the work of man. Lakes designed to store water for domestic and industrial use or to help provide energy by hydro-electric power stations are called reservoirs. Most natural lakes in Britain were formed by the action of Ice Age glaciers, and are found especially in Scotland, Wales and the Lake District. Lakes in such mountainous terrain are usually poor in mineral nutrients since the surrounding rocks are hard and do not wear down very easily to supply minerals to the water. These lakes, often in mountain corries (hollows in the rock), are called *oligotrophic* and have a few water plants and consequently not a great variety of animals. In the lowlands, on the other hand, the rocks are softer and lakes also receive chemical fertilisers draining away from surrounding farmland, so the mineral content of the waters is much higher. A luxuriant plant growth develops and often covers the lake with water lilies and other floating plants. Fish, insects and aquatic animals thrive in a rich environment described as *eutrophic*.

Seasons of the lake

Lakes are often virtually closed systems with little flow of water in or out. In summer the surface water becomes warm while the deeper water remains cold and dense and does not mingle with the upper layer. A distinct drop in temperature can be measured from the surface, where microscopic plant life (plant plankton) thrives, and the bottom of deep lakes. You will notice the presence of this temperature barrier or *thermocline* if you dive into a lake to swim. Floating at the surface can be warm, but it is much colder a few feet down. Dead plant and animal matter accumulates at the bottom, gradually decomposing and releasing nutrients which fail to mix with the upper waters where most plants and animals live. It is not until autumn and winter, when the surface cools, that the *thermocline* disappears and mixing of upper and lower waters takes place. Then nutrients become available at the surface and feed a new spring growth of plant life in the next year. So the annual cycle in the lake continues, controlling the seasons of aquatic life.

Lakes and Man

We all use many gallons of water every day: to drink, to cook our food in, to bath and wash and clean our teeth, to wash up, to wash our clothes. Every time we use the lavatory, two gallons of water are flushed away. Industry uses even greater quantities of water for cooling power stations, to provide steam, in chemical processes and to remove waste materials. Some towns and cities receive their water supply direct from lakes in mountain districts: water for Birmingham and the Midlands travels in pipes for many miles from the Welsh hills. But the largest natural lakes are in the west side of the country where there is greatest rainfall, yet many of our largest cities and greatest populations including London and the Home Counties, are on the eastern side. Water must therefore be supplied from artificially created lakes or reservoirs produced by building a large wall or dam across a valley, which is then allowed to flood. Many of our reservoirs were built in the last century or early years of the present century and are now inadequate to supply our water needs. Unfortunately much of our richest farm land is in south-east England and would be lost by creating new reservoirs there – new reservoirs have been constructed in recent times, but not only do they cost a great deal, they also arouse a great deal of controversy about the siting. When a vast reservoir was built in Upper Teesdale to supply the industry of Teesmouth, con-servationists and local residents protested at the destruction of an important natural site.

While mountain lakes may be difficult to reach for many people, a day spent at the local reservoir can be a much easier proposition. There is often good access for the wheelchair user, with paths across the main dam and around the margin. The reservoir provides diversity in the countryside: an aquatic environment where water may not naturally occur. Many recreational activities have been developed in recent years on our reservoirs – fishing, sailing, wind-surfing and nature trails. In addition, certain inaccessible areas of wet marshland, at the head of the reservoir, may be set aside as a local nature reserve, where wildlife can thrive free from interference from man. There are always interesting birds to see, since visitors from northern lands spend their winter on our lowland lakes. Ducks, geese and swans are typical of those arrivals from Greenland, Iceland, Scandinavia and Siberia. The yellow-billed Bewick's and Whooper Swans breed in the marshy tundra of northern

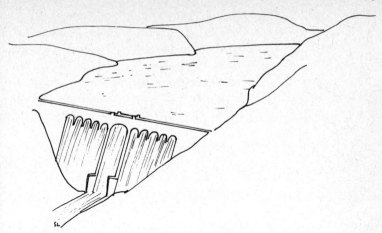

Fig. 6.16   A reservoir

latitudes, but journey south for the richer feeding grounds of our reservoirs. The attractive black and white smew, a saw-billed duck, makes a regular winter arrival on many London reservoirs, while grey geese from snowy lands fly south in V-shaped skeins to spend winter on reservoirs and coastal marshes. Wide variety of duck may be seen throughout much of the year – mallard and pochard, tufted and shoveler; some feeding at the water surface, others diving in search of food in deeper waters. The reservoir edge is home for moorhens and water rail, hiding among reeds at the water's margin. Pied and grey wagtails search for insects on the mud exposed by changing water levels, and many a rare spring and autumn migrating wader can be recorded on the local reservoir.

The view from the top of the dam, looking down on the continuous flow of cascading water, can be as exhilarating as seeing a mountain waterfall in the Scottish Highlands, and you may even be able to walk underneath the wall of water. Reservoirs are a perfect place to begin your study of water.

Canals
Britain's first canal was built by the Romans, but it was not until the eighteenth century that construction of our large system of over 4000 miles of inland waterways got under way. Transport

by barges was the principal way to supply the products of a
developing industry, and our major canals evolved in proximity
to industrial centres. The Trent and Mersey, Worcester and
Birmingham and the Grand Union all linked with major rivers
to serve rapidly growing inland cities. With the advent of the
railways in the following century there was a rapid decline in the
canal system, since steam trains provided a faster, cheaper
service, but still many canals survive today and it is possible to
travel from London to Liverpool on an inland waterway. In
more recent times the major ship canals were constructed, and
towards the end of the nineteenth century Queen Victoria
opened the great Manchester Ship Canal. Thus a route was
carved to provide a major industrial city with a direct connection to the sea, such that ships from countries far away could sail
direct to an inland port. In other parts of the world the Corinth,
Suez and Panama canals all opened up new routes for trade and
passage, shortening long journeys across the seas.

Much lore has developed around the life of the people of our
canals, and in the late nineteenth century almost thirty
thousand worked on the waterways – many actually on the
boats, others as 'navvies' who dug the ground for the channel of
the canal. The boats were long, narrow horse-drawn barges and
later steam tugs.

Canals and their towpaths are still to be found in many parts
today and have already developed a special relationship with
the handicapped. Canal holidays and daily excursions are
organised by Trusts with disabled people, and especially
wheelchair users, particularly well provided for. Thames cruises
on the traditional narrow boat *Battersea*, can be taken from
Radcot on the Thames in Oxfordshire. The boat, built in 1936
for the Grand Union Canal, was used for carrying cargoes
between London and the Midlands. Now its cargo can be groups
of disabled persons, out for a day to Lechlade or Oxford. The
boat can carry about eight or ten wheelchairs and is open-
planned. A passenger lift is installed and trips are organised for a
duration of two, three, five or eight hours.

The Peter le Marchant Trust has two boats, *Symphony* and
Sonata to provide free short holiday and day trips on waterways
to handicapped people. In 1981 a third boat joins the fleet. Once
again travel is on the Grand Union Canal, this time from

Loughborough. Both boats measure 70 feet and provide sufficient space for wheelchairs. Low windows give excellent vision and there is good access to toilets and showers. Hydraulic lifts and ramps enable easy boarding. Holidays between May and September are of three days, and in April and October day trips can be arranged in *Symphony*. *Sonata* is equipped for day cruising but not for longer holidays, and she carries about twelve handicapped plus helpers on particular days from April until October. Similar ventures are now available on other canals in the areas of Liverpool, Birmingham, Stoke-on-Trent, Macclesfield and on the Montgomery Canal. A new canal scheme is currently being organised in Stockport, and days on the canal are becoming a popular feature in the lives of many who are handicapped. Details of existing schemes can be obtained from the Peter le Marchant Trust, who may also be able to inform you of new local projects. The monthly magazine *Waterways World* also provides news and articles on canals past and present.

Coarse fishing

Freshwater fishing is one of the most popular of leisure activities and any stretch of water usually holds a stock of fish. Canals and rivers in large conurbations are a great attraction for the weekend angler, anxious to escape from city life. Lakes and reservoirs, disused gravel pits and large ponds are also suitable fishing sites where a variety of fish are to be caught. Indeed, the quarry of the coarse fisherman is any fish except trout, sea trout and salmon, for which a special licence is required. The still, weedy waters of ponds and lakes are the habitat preferred by carp and tench, the canal may harbour a shoal of perch clustered against a lock gate, while flowing river waters may yield a roach or rudd, chub or dace. It is important to learn about the popular fish of the waters you hope to fish – their haunts and habits, feeding and breeding – since in this way you will have better success with the sport. The local anglers, who regularly fish a favoured site, can tell you what they catch most often, and by watching their technique you will begin to learn how to use a rod and reel. Land is always owned by somebody and access to the river or lake, canal or pond may be restricted to members of an angling club which you will need to join. The River Boards and Water Authorities own and regulate fishing rights on many areas of water, including reservoirs. Find out where you are allowed to fish; whether the season has any restrictions; what licences you need; what are the local rules. It is always best to ask an experienced angler about these matters before you decide to purchase your own fishing tackle. Gradually you will learn about the equipment you need to fish yourself. A good general purpose rod may be purchased without great cost at a tackle shop or in many large chain stores. A good rod will last for years if well cared for, so buy the best you can afford. A fixed-spool reel is the correct type for float fishing, and nylon line of three pounds break-strain can be wound on to the reel. In addition there are several other items of tackle that you will need – floats, hooks, casts and weights; but these are much lower in cost than your rod and reel. You can probably get started for not much over £10 (1981 prices), although this will depend on the initial rod that you buy. Take as much advice as possible and see if someone will go with you to the tackle shop when choosing your equipment. You may be tempted to buy gear that is really unnecessary, or the incorrect choice for local waters.

Many anglers use live bait, maggots and worms, but bread can be just as good if correctly prepared. Put stale bread in a clean rag, soak in water, squeeze out all the water and knead the bread paste in your hands. A little flour added now will help to firm the paste. Pack your bait in a tin or used margarine container. When you are ready to fish, press a small piece of the paste on to your hook. Fish can be lured to an area where you intend to set up your rod by use of ground bait. A handful of dried crushed bread (use a mincer) mixed with cereal foods such as bran is highly suitable when scattered on the water. While fishing on a bank remain as quiet as possible, since fish can detect movement and vibrations transmitted through the water. They can also sense shadows cast over the water so be careful to watch the position of the sun. Sit by the water on a small stool and watch the water for fish before preparing your tackle away from the edge. If you are lucky enough to catch a fish, handle it carefully and be careful not to jerk the line suddenly free from the water or you may lose your first bite! Hold the rod well up and wind in carefully but do not lift the fish above the water. Rather, draw the catch through the water towards the bank so that it is not splashing about at the surface. Place your landing net beneath the fish and raise the net quickly but smoothly. Remove the hook with great care not to damage the fish, which you may wish to release back into the water. Coarse fish are not always good to eat, so never let a fish die slowly on the bank out of water. Handle the fish with damp hands or a piece of cloth, and let it gently slip back into the water. Removal of hooks takes skill and practice, so watch others more experienced than yourself, to begin with. You will more often than not return home without having made a catch, but the hours spent at the edge of the water will have given great pleasure and you will have seen a great deal of wildlife.

7. THE SEASHORE

Introduction

The holiday scene

Beach-combing

Making a shell collection

Pebbles on the beach

Animals of the sandy beach

Animals and plants of the shore

Seaweeds

Sponges, anemones and worms

Snails, crabs and urchins

Fish

Seawater aquaria

Fish and fishing

Exploring the coastline – seabirds and cliff walks

Sand dunes

Estuaries and salt marsh

7. THE SEASHORE

Introduction
Some people are fortunate enough to live at the coast and visit the sea when they wish, but for most of us a visit to the seaside is something rare and special. So it needs to be made the most of. It is not enough merely to take a handicapped person to the sea, and let him look on from afar; we should use the opportunity in a much more positive way. So in this chapter we suggest how the handicapped child can become involved in planning the holiday, and then how she can herself investigate the world at the edge of the shore, and make collections of shells, pebbles and other finds from the strandline. Digging holes in the sandy beach may yield animals when the tide retreats, and we find out more about their lives and of the birds that feed upon them. Everyone loves to collect in rock pools, to see crabs, anemones and prawns, and slide about on the damp seaweeds. We learn how these tidal animals and plants survive the rigours of a marine existence and how they can be kept in a home aquarium. Harbours and quays are good to visit and seafishing can yield your evening supper, as well as occupy a pleasant day for the disabled angler. Finally we leave the shore to search the world of cliffs, sand dunes and salt marsh, looking at birds, insects and flowers.

The Holiday Scene
For the town and city dweller, preparation for a holiday at the seaside can be an exciting part of the treat. Where shall we go? Brochures arrive, full of glossy pictures. Shall we go by rail or take the car? The house becomes alive in the evening as the holiday takes shape. This is one of the principal occasions for decision, organisation and enjoyment in the lives of most of us: more money is spent on the holiday than on any other regular event in the year, yet it can turn out a success – or a disaster. Factors we can't control, the weather, our health – can be critical.

Clearly there are additional complications to arranging a holiday when in addition there is a handicapped member of the family. There may be embarrassment over behavioural problems or incontinence, and when a wheelchair is involved access must be considered. A self-catering holiday may be the answer, although many hotels and guest houses are now adapted to provide facilities for the disabled, including ramps, lifts, downstairs bedrooms, wider doors, adapted toilets and bathrooms. Many have been assisted by the English Tourist Board, who publish annual lists of holiday accommodation indicating places suitable for wheelchairs.

Voluntary organisations such as The Spastics Society have hotels and other styles of accommodation which provide specifically for the disabled. Further afield, in the Channel Isles the Maison de Landes at St Ouen, Jersey, a hotel set amidst sandy beaches and dunes in an idyllic situation, is specifically designed with the comfort of disabled people in mind. And Local Tourist Boards also advise and produce their own publications. The newly formed Holiday Care Service has been established to provide information on holiday opportunities for disabled people.

While the handicapped child may not be able to take an active part in the holiday arrangements, there are ways in which anticipation can be used to educational advantage. The mentally handicapped young person can find pleasure in building a scrap book based on pictures from holiday brochures and at the same time gain an insight into what to expect in the new environment. Sea, sand, sunshine become apparent from pictures. Deck chairs and swimming, bright lights and crowds of people – all are new and potentially exciting. The more able child will be able to find out for himself about the holiday area, where it is and the best way of getting there. Once again, a great deal of normal school curriculum can be dealt with in greater depth than might otherwise seem possible by taking advantage of the right situation. Involvement is important at all levels and the handicapped child should not feel or be excluded. For the school-leaver or adult especially, perhaps confined to home and living without the involvement of work, time can drag slowly. So rather than let it be here and gone again in a week or two, the

holiday should be allowed to occupy and stimulate over as long
a period as possible. It may be one of the few events in the year to
which a handicapped person can look forward with unalloyed
delight.

WHEELCHAIRS:
Sand is not the ideal ground surface for wheelchairs. There is no
easy way to move a wheelchair over soft surfaces. But it is far
better to pull than to push, since pulling prevents the small front
wheels from binding into the sand. Tilting the wheelchair on to
the back wheels also helps remove drag and can ·make
movement easier, but for certain kinds of handicap this is not
possible or desirable. The person moving the chair also needs to
be confident of this technique to avoid disaster. However, some
local beaches are easier than others, especially if they have a slip-
way for boats from the road, or a path down to the sea. A harder
surface is found on a beach with shingle at the top, and this may
help the wheelchair user. Once on the beach it may be possible
to dispense with the wheelchair, but in some instances the
individual will have to remain where positioned.

Beach-combing

The upper beach provides both play and educational possibi-
lities. Pebbles and shells, shingle and sand offer experience of
texture, shape and colour. Beachcombing is fun for all. There is
always the element of excitement and discovery, and the desire
to collect is inborn in man. Debris washed up by the last high
tide forms a distinct strand-line of seaweed, wood and polythene
waste. As many types of seaweed can often be found there as
down among the rock pools where they normally grow: large
kelps from the deeper sea mix with more delicate green and red
forms. These can be floated on a small dish of water (the lid of
the packed lunch box will do) to show the natural beauty and
colour of many species. Small seaweeds can then be transferred
from water to paper, again allowing them to float so that they lie
flat. Excess water is drained off and the seaweed dried beneath
tissue paper and a heavy book. Their natural slimy surface sticks
them securely. As a permanent collection, they can be arranged
in patterns, a popular craft in Victorian times, or labelled and
categorised. Driftwood and large pebbles, rubbed smooth by
constant wave action, also provide a range of texture and shape,

Fig. 7.1 Beachcombing: a. tower shell b. kelps c. mussel d. winkles e. dogfish eggcase f. razor shell g. scallop h. dog whelk i. cuttle bone j. wracks k. whelk eggcase l. skate eggcase m. sea urchin

and tell their own story. They can be examined on the beach or taken home to be painted, placed on a shelf or used in a variety of ways, such as in flower arrangements or as lamp stands. Polythene is virtually indestructible, and survives long journeys at sea. Containers may be labelled in a strange language, thrown away by foreign ships and carried ashore. Other objects found may not be so easy to identify, especially remnants of animals of the deep sea.

Flat, white, oval 'bones' about six inches long are really the remains of the internal shell of the cuttlefish, a close relative of the octopus. Strange horny shapes with distinct points at each corner, often called 'Mermaid's Purses', are the empty egg cases of dogfish and rays, fish related to sharks. Those of the dogfish have coiled tendrils at each corner, resembling the growing climbing shoots of pea plants. Often the 'purse' is black and dried and perfectly suitable for a collection of drift matter glued on card. Such a collection develops a whole range of skills: observation, collection, identification and the grouping of like materials into sets. A simple key for identification of drift matter can be constructed which the slow-learning child could use. The basis of the key might be the manner by which the material arrived on the beach as 'flotsam' or 'jetsam' – or the more natural division of 'animal', 'vegetable' or 'mineral'.

Making a shell collection

This is a pastime adaptable to both mentally and physically handicapped people. Shells are usually to be found near the top of the beach, convenient for the wheelchair user, and most resorts have good shell beaches.

Collecting also does not produce a conservation dilemma, since the animal (a *mollusc*) originally occupying the shell is now dead. Shells are often bright, attractive, tough and easy to handle – except for a few more delicate types. They do not evoke an 'Ugh' when placed in the hand! The collection for the day can be taken away from the beach and will travel easily home at the end of the holiday. It will give hours of enjoyment simply in looking at and playing with them, sorting and classifying.

On the beach, try to be selective, especially if the shells are going into a permanent collection. Discard damaged ones and collect them in rigid plastic kitchen containers (margarine and ice cream tubs are very suitable). Wrap delicate shells in a piece of tissue. Before further work on them; the shells should be washed under a tap to remove sand, and if necessary gently scrubbed with an old toothbrush. The collector will then want to name his finds. There are several good reference books with colour plates, and more popular books based on the shells of particular regions, such as Cornwall. The local museum may also have a named collection. There are about six hundred varieties of marine shell to be found in Britain, so the hobby can

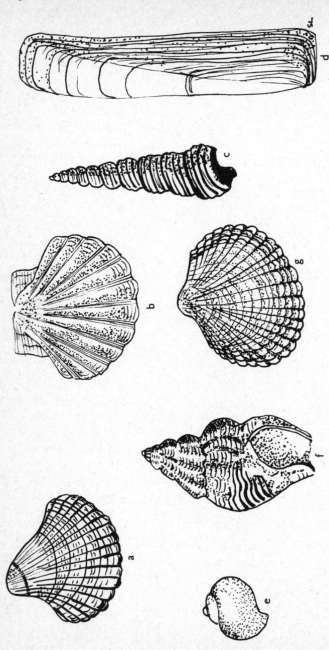

Fig. 7.2   Some shells of the beach: a. cockle   b. scallop   c. tower shell   d. razor shell   e. flat periwinkle   f. dogwhelk   g. venus shell

progress over many years. Identification is based on size, shape, colour, shell thickness and markings; but beware of worn shell surfaces and size variation due to age. Most shells will fall into one of two categories, the univalves (whelks, periwinkles) with a single shell which is normally coiled into whorls, or the bivalves (mussels, cockles) with two joined parts or valves to the shell.

Display your shells by fixing with a clear glue to a small piece of white card on which the popular name, date and locality is written with a fine fibretip pen. The shell can be given a thin coat of a clear lacquer or varnish from a spraycan if you want a real, professional finish, but this is not necessary. Storage is the greater problem since ideally shells are best kept under glass in drawers or in a large box with a cork base. However, a simple and cheap method is to use a large cardboard box (a shoe box) cut down to a depth of two inches. Cut a polystyrene ceiling tile to size and place in the bottom as a base to which you can pin your card-mounted shells. The top can be the original box lid, or if you want a 'clear view' top stretch a piece of cling-film across the box when it is full of shells. There should be no problem if the shells are clean and dry when mounted, but a small mothball could be inserted to deter pests. The beauty of using shoe boxes is that they are easily obtained and are of standard size and shape for storage in a cupboard or on a shelf. The collection can be based on one locality (your local holiday resort); or you can use a different box for each place. Alternatively your shells can be arranged according to the classification system used in one of the books listed.

Pebbles on the beach

Who has failed to enjoy sitting by the side of the sea tossing pebbles into the waves or skimming flat ones across the surface of the water? It is a pastime that can occupy most children, and often adults, for hours and the pleasure derived from it is difficult to describe. The shape, size, colour and feel of the pebbles; choosing some, discarding others; the distance you can throw them; pitching them into a breaking wave, and the inevitable 'splash' are all part of it. Yet it is a pleasure which strangely seems to have been denied many handicapped children, not necessarily because of the disability but because no one thought about it. I remember a bright boy with spina bifida and an incredible degree of independence, of an age soon to leave school, to whom I introduced the fun of skimming stones by accident, and the excitement we shared. Is it important? I believe it is. Not only should learning be fun, it should be physical as well as cerebral, and it is important that the handicapped should not miss out on such basic experiences.

Pebbles, like shells, can be collected, or used for craft work. But there are also a great many questions about them to be answered. How did they come to be there, how to account for differences in shape and colour, in texture and composition? We are entering here the realms of geology, the world of rocks and minerals, the quest for semi-precious stones. There are plenty of books to provide basic identification of granite and flint, sandstone and schist pebbles; and guides to good places for search – the Lizard in Cornwall for serpentine in beautiful reds and greens, or Whitby on the Yorkshire coast for black jet, for instance. If you want to find amethysts and agates, you will have to make deliberate journeys and an even more exacting hunt, but the ordinary pebble will form the basis of an interesting collection and leisure activity. Collecting invariably leads on to a thirst for further information, and before long it becomes compulsive.

Pebbles can be stored as they are found, in a drawer unit made from matchboxes for smaller specimens and in shoe boxes arranged as for a shell collection for larger stones. Small self-adhesive labels fixed to the pebble will provide information on the type of pebble, locality and date. For a more polished appearance the amateur geologist must enter the field of *lapidary*. Many towns have craft shops which specialise in equipment for the home-jewelry maker. A small tumbler unit is relatively cheap to purchase and operate, and small pebbles reveal an infinite range of colours and markings when polished. Polishing and handling stones you have found yourself is a perfect activity for cold, wet winter evenings, and makes a satisfying link between an environmental-based out-of-door activity and an indoor hobby.

Both shells and pebbles are perfect natural materials for craft work. It is not within the scope of this book to give details of such skills, but shells can be made into small animal figures using a clear glue to fix small shell 'eyes' to a larger shell 'body'. They can be embedded in a stiff plaster of Paris coating over a bottle, which can then form a base for a bedside light, or over a small wood box which will later hold trinkets and valuables. Intricate patterns can be made, using shells of a particular type or colour. Pebbles can be combined with shells in all of these ways or can be used alone. Polished pebbles can be mounted in rings, brooches and pendants. The metal clasps and chains can be bought very cheaply from craft shops and suppliers. The complete lapidarist will want eventually to take the hobby further and look inside his finds. Stones can be cut with special discs, after which the inner surface should be finely ground and polished. In this way thin sections can be removed from the centre of the pebble, polished on both sides to allow light to pass through, and reveal the composition, pattern and colour of the stone.

Animals of the sandy beach

Walking along the sea edge at low tide, the gentle movement of the water against your feet, you may not notice much sign of animal life down among the sand. And indeed the large expanses of beach on the west coast of Britain are not the places to find a variety of marine life, since the sand is cleaned too effectively of debris by the action of the waves. But if you search the sheltered coves and bays, you will find the circular casts of the lugworm and the delicate tubes and shells of other worms and molluscs. All of our shores are subject to the twice-daily cycle of ebb and flow of the tides, with approximately six hours between high and low water. At high tide the animals are covered by the sea and move to the sand surface where they feed with intricate mechanisms to trap minute particles of debris. Many, like the fan worms, are very attractive but are seldom seen except in the marine aquarium. As the tide recedes, the animals must retreat back into their sand lairs to avoid the drying effects of sun and the probing beaks of many seabirds. Even on the busy beaches, gulls will search for shell-life at the edge of the tide but it is to the quiet beach that we must go to see the white sanderling running to and fro at the water's edge, dunlin, sandpiper, turnstone, oystercatcher and other wading birds. All have bills of different length, to allow them to explore the sand, and probe for worms, crustaceans and molluscs at different depths, and so avoid competing for the same food. A

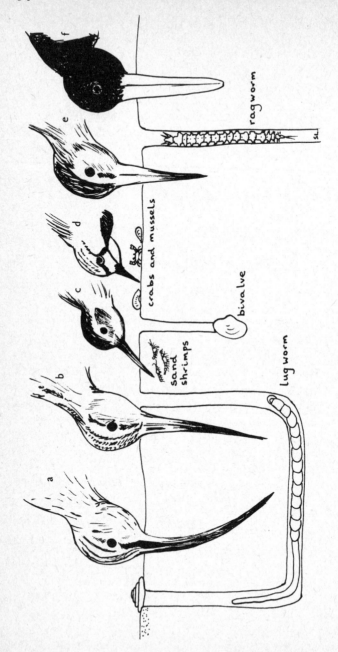

Fig. 7.3 Feeding adaptations of seashore wading birds: a. curlew b. godwit c. dunlin d. turnstone e. redshank f. oystercatcher

gathering of large numbers of waders indicates a good variety of marine life, so the beach is worthy of a dig.

Take a bucket and a spade or fork, even the childrens' metal bucket and spade, and search the sand depths for the more common ragworms and lugworm, cockles and razor shells or the

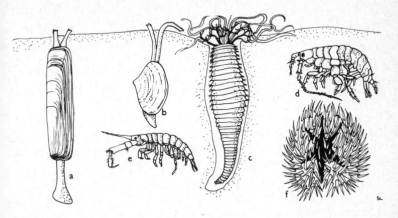

Fig. 7.4   Life in the sand: a. razor shell   b. tellin shell   c. bristleworm   d/e sand shrimps   f. heart urchin

rare heart urchin and burying starfish. Collected alive they can be observed in seawater in the bucket. The ragworm has bright, irridescent colours and paddles along either side of its body. The cockle has a pink muscular foot, used for burrowing rapidly down in the sand. Look also for the thin valves of the wedge shells and the soft golden coloured spines of the heart urchin. Leave them behind at the water's edge and they will rapidly disappear again into their world of sand.

The rock pool – tides and shore life
Nothing is so appealing to both children and adults on holiday at the seaside as paddling about in rock pools as the tide retreats. Turning stones and seaweeds or fishing with a small net from the local beach shop reveals a whole new world left behind by the sea. The rock pool is in itself a miniature sea – a natural aquarium. At high tide it will flood and release its captive animals to the mercy of the waves, but at low tide it is as much

part of the land environment as it is of the sea. Water in the pool becomes warm under the summer sun and the natural salt content increases as water evaporates away. On rainy days the salinity falls as fresh water mixes with the salty sea water. Consequently animals inhabiting rock pools must be able to cope with changes in temperature and salinity in their environment. Many seek shelter under seaweeds or stones, in crevices or under overhanging rocks, and it is in these places that we must search for them. Seaweeds too will loose water if they are exposed to the drying influence of the sun and wind, and only those which are tough and able to cope with this problem of dessication can be found growing at the edge of the rocky shore. More delicate seaweeds must grow inside the pools or in the lower regions of the shore, where the tide leaves them uncovered for much shorter periods. The slimy nature of seaweeds assists them in their survival by retaining moisture in a layer of mucus around the plant. When the tide once again covers them they can reabsorb water rapidly and resume their naturally soft and pliable form.

Although each day the tide rises and falls twice, the actual time of each tide is not constant. Each day the time of high water is slightly later, generally by half to one hour. Tide times for different places can be found in local papers, or in specially published tidetables. Collecting from rock pools is more product-ive during spring tides when the tidal range between high and low water is greatest. These occur every month, not only in spring, but the most spectacular spring tides occur for a few days in spring, usually March, and autumn, usually September. During the remainder of the month the tidal range is less: such tides are called neap tides, and leave less of the rocky shore uncovered at low tide.

The seashore consequently can be divided into a number of zones, from the high water line of spring tides down to the margin of the sea at low water during spring tides. Each zone is typified by different seaweeds and shore animals, but since many animals can move about, crawling or swimming, they may be found throughout the full range of the shore.

Thus, seaweeds and sedentary animals like limpets, anem-ones, barnacles and mussels are the best to use to identify each zone of the rocky shore. These are not scattered at random across the shore but each variously adapted to life when the tide retreats. Species which will tolerate long periods of exposure can be found high up on the shore. More delicate species must live in the pools or low down at the edge of the sea. Wave action also affects the distribution of species on some shores, and many exposed rocky shores, such as those on the open Atlantic, have less biological variety: they are typified by barnacles, limpets and mussels, with few seaweeds except in the occasional pools. The most luxuriant shores are in sheltered coves or, in Scotland, on the margins of inland sea lochs. There, seaweeds grow to great lengths and form dense carpets, and more delicate animals, normally found only in deeper waters, can survive in their tangled mat.

Animals and plants of the shore

If we begin our walk at the top of the shore, in the 'splash zone' above high water mark, we are in a transitional environment between land and sea. It is often possible to take a child confined to a wheelchair into this region of the shore, to introduce her to the world of sea spray. Patches of bright orange and yellow usually encrust the rocks. This is the lichen *Xanthoria*, and elsewhere we may find black, tar-like patches denoting *Verrucaria* or grey tufted growths, often quite dry and brittle to touch which are the growths of *Ramalina*. Lichens unfortunately do not have common names, but they are interesting primitive plants, each consisting in part of an alga and in part of a fungus. They form a suitable collection but most need to be removed with a small piece of substrate-rock, wood or other matter. They are best kept dry in envelopes or stuck on to card and stored in a box. While identification is very difficult, they are beautiful to observe, especially under a lens or microscope.

Scattered among the lichens are tufts of the sea pink or thrift, the strongly aromatic rock samphire or the small fleshy leaves of English stone-crop – for some flowering plants can also resist the effects of salt spray on their leaves. Few animals inhabit this region of the shore. Sea slaters, resembling overgrown woodlice, hide in crevices and the occasional insect runs about among the boulders. Here, rock pools may be touched by the sea only once or twice a year and the water stagnates, turning green and slimy from growths of algae. Salt often encrusts the margins of such pools and green weeds become bleached by the sun.

Seaweeds:
Following the retreating tide we see immediately the dense growths of brown seaweeds or 'wracks' which cover the shore

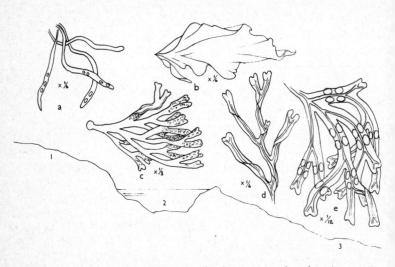

Fig. 7.5   The pattern of seaweeds down a rocky shore: a. gut weed   b. sea lettuce   c. channelled wrack   d. spiral wrack   e. bladder   f. knotted wrack   g. saw wrack   h. red weed   i. sea oak   j. kelps (1. upper shore;   2. high water pool;   3. Mid-shore;   4. low water pool;   5. lower shore)

from high to low water. Seaweeds are the most complex and highly developed algae. Different species dominate each zone, the channelled wrack and spiral wrack forming tufts on rocks in the upper shore, while the bladder and knotted wrack form a dense blanket over the mid-shore. The lower shore is dominated by the serrated or saw wrack, and the lowest margins by the large 'kelps'. While brown seaweeds certainly cover most of the shore, not all are this colour. Green slimy patches of *Enteromorpha* appear among the brown carpet and the sea lettuce, *Ulva*, can be found at all levels of the shore. In deeper pools and at the lowest part of the shore red seaweeds abound in variety, some tough and leathery, others delicate and translucent. All seaweeds are green underneath their surface colour, a fact which is easily shown by dropping a portion into a suitable solvent such as alcohol or methylated spirits. The brown or red seaweed rapidly turns green and this green pigment, chlorophyll, may colour the solvent. Without it the plant would not be able to absorb sunlight from above the water and produce its own sugar foodstuffs. Light is essential for seaweeds, as for other plants, and the air-bladders found on wracks in the mid-shore, which 'pop' when dry and pressed between fingers, enable the large fronds of

weed to float near the surface – and thus near the light. The red pigment enables lower intensity light to be utilised by red seaweeds growing in deep pools, or even beneath the sea in parts not uncovered by the tide.

Sponges, anemones and worms:
Animals of the seashore are mainly *invertebrates* (without a

backbone) and represent most of the major groups of animal classification except for insects. Life began in the sea, and the seashore reveals a variety of forms. Many look like plants; others look like nothing living at all!

Yellow, green or orange sponges may encrust the underside of overhanging rock crevices. Jelly-like 'blobs' adhering to rocks, coloured reds, brown or green, are beadlet anemones, close relatives of the corals and jellyfish. They assume a more attractive shape when submerged in a rock pool, a circle of tentacles surrounding the mouth, awaiting their prey. Drop a small piece of mussel or limpet on to these tentacles and watch the immediate reaction as they push the food from view into an engulfing mouth. The larger, green snakelocks anemones have long, waving tentacles (each resembling a snake) while the flower-like dahlia anemone has a crown of short, pointed, brightly coloured tentacles. Some bury themselves in sand in the bottom of pools and are detectable only from the tips of their tentacles.

Worms live in tubes made of sand, gravel or lime. Tiny white spiral tubes found especially on serrated wrack are the homes of the tube worm, *Spirorbis*, while the white limy tubes of *Pomatoceros* can be found encrusting stones and boulders. Place such a stone under water in a pool and watch the entrance to the tube through a lens. Soon a circlet of translucent tentacles appears and waves in the water, trapping small particles of food to be ingested by the worm. Such filter feeding is a common feature of marine sedentary animals.

Snails, crabs and urchins:
But it is to the shell-fish that we turn for the widest variety of inter-tidal animals. A shell forms a protective cover for molluscs (limpets, sea snails, mussels), crustacea (barnacles, crabs, prawns, shrimps, lobsters) and echinoderms (sea urchins, starfish). Limpets are conspicuous on all shores, sticking tight to rocks. They are difficult to remove, and you must give them a sudden knock if you want to see the underside, where a huge muscular foot covers the entrance to the shell. Most molluscs are plant eaters, browsing on the algae that cover the shore, but the dog whelks are carnivorous, feeding on barnacles and mussels. Periwinkles and top shells are common under seaweeds and in

pools. They move about at hightide and close their shells with a horny cover on the foot when the tide is out. Patrons of the whelk stall use a bent pin to 'winkle out' the whelk or periwinkle from behind this cover. Sea slugs have no obvious shell but are cousins to the sea snails. They are often brightly coloured – yellow, orange, red, purple – and are adorned by fringes and circles of tentacles, folds of skin or warts. Long, tubular processes may extend from their backs making them among the most attractive of marine creatures (totally unlike their garden relatives).

The great majority of varieties of crustacea live in the sea. Numerous crab species – the shore, edible, spider, hermit, soldier, swimming, fiddler and porcelain crabs – are to be found on a good rocky shore. Squat lobsters, prawns, shrimps and slaters of wide variety abound, and every shoreline has its' cover of barnacles, also of several types. While superficially these species do not always look as though they are related, they all show similar development, and young barnacles and crabs, for instance, look very similar. Finding a crab under a stone or weed always causes excitement, as it scuttles away sideways with front claws held aloft. Hermit crabs inhabit the old shells of snails, with only their hard claws protruding. As they grow they must regularly leave one shell for a larger one, and while they are 'moving house' they are specially vulnerable to predators, since their body is soft and unprotected. Translucent prawns dart backwards when they are disturbed. Like shrimps, crabs and lobsters they are only bright pink when boiled. Crustacea are scavengers on the shore, and even the small barnacles, living inside their hard, white shells, and often looking scarcely alive, feed at high tide by kicking their legs through the open shell and combing out small food particles.

Sea urchins and starfish both have prickly skin, but in the urchin the spines drop away from the underlying shell when the creature dies, leaving behind the typical form that we know from the shell and craft shop. In life the spines can move. The urchin moves about on small sucker-like tubefeet browsing on young seaweeds. Starfish, brittle stars, sun stars and cushion stars generally have five arms and a very horny, spiny skin. They are carnivores; the common starfish pulls apart the two shell valves of mussels with its arms, then devours the contents.

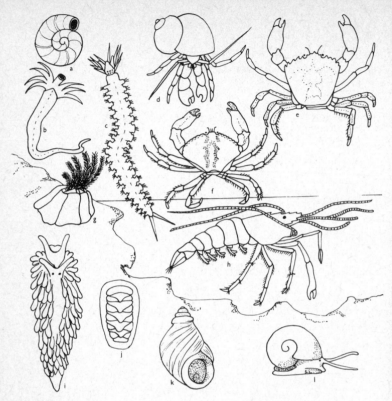

Fig. 7.6 The world of the rock pool: a. tube worm   b. keel worm   c. ragworm   d. hermit crab   e. shore crab   f. edible crab   g. barnacle   h. prawn   i. sea slug   j. chiton   k. common winkle   l. flat periwinkle   m. sponge   n. beadlet anemone   o. brittlestar   p. snakelocks anemone   q. cushion star   r. starfish   s. sea urchin   t. limpet   u. dogwhelk   v. top shell   w. blenny   x. goby

Fish:

Fish are familiar animals to us all, and while some are species of the shore, others found in rock pools are in fact, the young of fish that normally live in deeper waters: young mullet and wrasse can be seen alongside anemones and limpets. But the most common rock pool fish are blennies and gobies, sandy in colour, living near the bottom of the pool and often difficult to see. Also to be found is the shore rockling, with small barbels, like

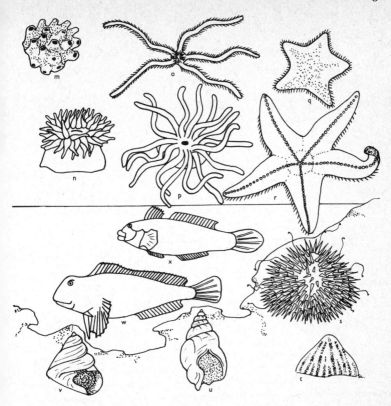

tentacles, around its mouth; the scorpion fish covered with venomous spines on fin and gill covers to give it its horrifying appearance; and the slippery butterfish, its body flattened sideways and dark markings along the length of its upper surface. A snake-like creature is probably a pipefish, with minute fins; or a sea stickleback, with fifteen spines along its back and long drawn-out tail. The flattened sucker fish clings to rocks against the tide, with suckers formed from modified fins. All these can be caught in a rock pool with a simple net and a little patience.

Seawater aquaria
Marine animals are seldom kept by the amateur aquarist, but families who live within easy reach of the sea, and schools with the necessary resources may be able to set up a marine

aquarium. Seawater can be made artificially from a formula in a
relevant book, but generally this is impracticable, and we will
assume that natural sea water can be obtained in quantity.
Water is heavy and several journeys may be required to fill the
tank. Seawater is also highly corrosive, so a metal framed
aquarium will certainly rust unless treated along the joints and
metal surfaces with several coats of non-contaminating paint
such as Bituros. Joints between the glass sheets require a layer of
Glasticon, pressed into place with a finger, to prevent the
seawater from seeping through to the metal.

Plastic and all-glass moulded tanks can be bought, but it is
possible to use other types of containers, including food
containers available from hardware stores. Tanks made at home
from wood can be efficient, cheap and strong. Instructions are
available in Jackman's *Seawater Aquaria* (see book list) for
making a tank with parana pine or marine ply, joined together

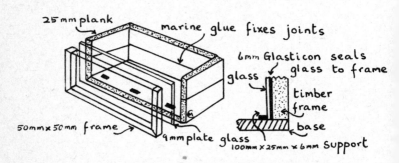

Fig. 7.7   Making a marine aquarium (after Jackman 1974)

with marine glues. The powdered resin-based glue is mixed with
cold water and applied to one surface and the transparent
hardener to the other. When the two surfaces are brought
together a perfect watertight joint results, which is exceedingly
strong. There is no need for special jointing, simply butt
together the two cut surfaces. Tanks up to 2′ long require pine
25mm (1″ thick as a base and 20mm–25mm ($\frac{3}{4}$″–1″) thick for the
three sides. Select good timber free from holes, cracks or other
faults where water could leak, and work on it immediately,
before it has a chance to warp. The front should be 10mm ($\frac{3}{8}$″)
plate glass, cut at your local shop, sealed to the timber frame

with a 6mm ($\frac{1}{4}''$) layer of Glasticon. Paint the finished tank with black non-contaminating bituminous paint such as Bituros, and you are nearly ready to collect your specimens.

First design the inside of your aquarium to create the correct environment for each animal. Select rocks and pebbles to produce crevices and caves for shelter, a few old seashells for worms to hide in and a clean sand bed about 6mm ($\frac{1}{4}''$) deep to cover the floor. Do not use sand which is too fine or it will cloud the water, or too deep a layer as this will encourage black smelly deposits where oxygen has not reached. A well balanced tank requires the sand to be removed for washing only once a year – not every week. Finally the tank must be aerated and the water circulated and filtered. Small circulation pumps suitable for seawater can be bought quite cheaply from a good pet shop or aquarists' store. The water is circulated through a filter pack or box containing glass wool and charcoal. Place 25mm ($1''$) glass wool over the bottom of the filter, add 25mm ($1''$) charcoal granules (not powder) and cover with a further layer of glass wool. The glass wool needs to be changed about every fortnight and the charcoal after one or two months. The circulation ensures that cleansed water is returning to your tank and leaves behind all impurities in the filter pack. Filter pumps need not run all day and night: four- or five-hour spells should be enough. Aearation can be provided by attaching a diffusion stone by rubber or plastic tubing to your pump, and hiding it behind a rock or inside a large shell. Regulate the supply of air with a small clamp attached to the tubing to give a good steady stream of bubbles without causing disturbances to the sandy bottom. Plastic junctions can be bought with your tubing and diffusion stone to attach both the filtration and aeration system to the pump. Tank maintenance should be minimal if your system is well balanced and you do not overfeed the animals.

The animals, but not the seaweeds, collected on your holiday can now be introduced into your own rock pool. Do not be too ambitious to start with, and use a few well selected animals rather than hundreds of periwinkles and crabs. Try to create a balanced system, a few filter-feeders (mussels, tube worms, barnacles, seasquirts), some bottom scavengers (a small crab, hermit crabs), some herbivores (a limpet, periwinkles, top shells, sea urchin) and carnivores (sea anemones, a starfish and some fish). Small specimens are often more successful than large – remember that one big crab can grow larger in your tank by eating everything else! Position your aquarium in a cool, shaded part of the room away from large windows and you will have hours of entertainment watching the life of the sea creatures.

Feeding two or three times each week is sufficient, and you will develop more trouble by overfeeding than by underfeeding. A good fresh food for the inland aquarist is white fish such as whiting or gurnard, cut into very small pieces and washed before placing in the tank. Your greatest problem will be decay of animal or vegetable matter – a tank can soon begin to smell and the water turn cloudy – so remove any uneaten food about two hours after feeding. Similarly if one of your animals dies remove it immediately. If you are unsure whether it is dead or not, take it out of the tank anyway and put it in a separate container of seawater to observe for a few hours for any signs of life. Better to be safe than sorry!

Fish and fishing

A visit to the fish shop before the holiday will introduce a child to the appearance of a variety of fish. Many seaside holiday towns have fish markets, which are always exciting places to look around as the fish are removed from their ice boxes and displayed on white marble slabs. Often fish not usually seen in the local shop window appear – dogfish, skate and rays – and a whole cod is a real surprise to someone who has only seen a portion surrounded by batter in a fish and chip supper! Fish and fishing are an important part of the holiday, especially if there is a local harbour. Watch the fishing boats come in and unload their cargoes, the nets and equipment on board, the fishermen and their appearance and clothes. Auctions are often held alongside the harbour, vans and lorries load and take the fish to local and city markets. Fishing museums, perhaps in old harbourside buildings, depict the history of the local fishing industry – old techniques and equipment, changes in fish caught, in the people and harbour scene.

Sea fishing is relatively easy to succeed at, even for the wheelchair user. Rod and line from the pier or harbour wall may land pollack or whiting, but also the more humble hand line, baited with sand eels or pieces of shell fish, will usually tempt a mackeral in summer time in most seaside holiday districts. A hand line is of limited use from harbours and piers, however, because more often than not a crab will appear on the end of the line! Crabs can, however, be useful for bait, especially the soft 'peelers', at the stage of growing a new shell. The line is a stout nylon twine, weighted at the end, with one or more thin nylon

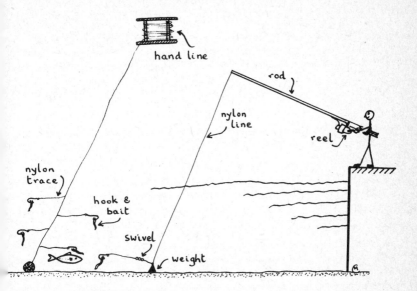

Fig. 7.8 Seafishing tackle

traces bearing hooks attached above the weight. Suitable bait can be found in rock pools, dug out of the sand at low tide, or bought from a local tackle shop.

Sand eels are especially good, but mackerel strips are also suitable for catching mackerel. This is best done from a boat, so a slight modification of the tackle has to be made, by inserting a spinner with hooks in place of the weight and traces. The spinner attracts the mackerel when it is pulled through the water behind a boat. Hand line, weights, swivel, spinner and hooks can all be purchased for about two pounds.

The young fisherman on holiday, however, will soon want to try a rod when he sees other anglers alongside on the harbour wall pulling in larger and different fish. This need not be

expensive to begin with, and could provide a life-long recreational activity. A light rod is important, not too long, and it
must be bought for the person who is going to use it. Each
individual will have different abilities and requirements. In
general a light sea or freshwater rod, about 2.50 to 3m (8–10 feet)
long and with a fixed spool reel is suitable, and can then also be
used at home for coarse fishing in pond, lake, canal, or river.
Tackle for seafishing can be simple – a light sea float attached to
the nylon line (about 4 kilo – 10lb. – breaking-strain), weighted
with a few split shot, and baited hook at the end can be used
from the harbour or off the rocks where bass and other fish can
be caught. The complete system may be bought for about £10
(1981 prices) although the figure could be much higher if your
demands are greater. You can buy a kit from a tackle shop, but
you would do better to buy your equipment separately and have
a rod that suits your own needs.

The handicapped person unable to hold a rod may find that
an adaptation can be attached to the wheelchair to take the rod
weight after casting. Often the best adaptation is simple and
suits the individual. The National Anglers' Council (see Resources list) produces a booklet on opportunities for Disabled
Anglers and there is also an excellent film, *Sea Fishing for the
Disabled* released by the Disabled Living Foundation. There are
many information books on sea fishing, and local Angling
Guides available from Tourist Boards, an excellent example
being the *Angling Guide to Wales* published by the Wales Tourist
Board. Angling is said to be the most popular recreation in
Britain, and young fanatics might consider joining a specialist
club such as the Kingfisher Guild, or the local angling club.

Exploring the coastline – seabirds and cliff walks
Although the sandy beach and rocky shore may occupy most of
your holiday, they are not the only places to visit. There is a
refreshing wildness about our coastal scenery, cliff tops and sand
dunes, salt marshes and estuaries. You can explore by car along
the coast road and often see a great deal of wildlife in this way.
Seabirds soar along a cliff edge on rising air currents, nesting on
narrow rock ledges in inaccessible places or on small offshore
islands. Colonies of auks, razorbills and guillemots: and fulmars,
with their strange tube-nose which drips a concentrated salt

Fig. 7.9 Fish-eating seabirds: a. herring gull b. cormorant
c. tern d. fulmar e. razorbill f. shag g. puffin
h. gannet

solution, cluster round the rocks. Their white droppings are
everywhere, with the characteristic smell produced by fish-
eating birds, and the noise is sometimes so loud that it is
impossible to hear yourself speak amid the constant coming and
going from the colony as birds depart for more food at sea, and
return to supply ever-open mouths. Even a single nesting fulmar
on the cliff will provide hours of delighted watching as it soars
about with stiff, outstretched wings resembling a glider, landing
effortlessly on the mounded nest. If you are lucky gannets, with a
two-metre wingspan, may be spotted diving at sea from great
heights, their black-tipped wings held close against a snow-white
body: no other sea bird can produce such a spectacular display.
Gulls are always present, even at the most popular resort, and on
a quiet coastal stretch you may see the smaller species of kittiwake
in colonies of close-nesting birds, each nest constructed from
green seaweed stuck to the cliff with mud. Kittiwakes nest in busy
city places too, on harbour buildings where window sills substi-
tute for cliff ledges. The most common seaside gull is the herring
gull, a larger species, which also nests on buildings, having a
preference for roof tops, as well as its native cliffs. Herring gulls,
Great and Lesser Black-backed gulls and Black-headed gulls are
all common in summer around most of our coast and can easily
be tempted with the remains of your picnic. Good quality

photographs have often been taken by feeding gulls from the open car window in the seaside car park.

Many flowers growing on sea cliffs can also be found inland, but some are restricted to the coast, flourishing only within reach of the salt spray. Maritime plants like thrift and sea campion grow mixed with typical inland flowers such as bluebells, red campion or even foxgloves. In some western areas the cliffs are a carpet of gorse, heathers and bracken fern, more reminiscent of moorland vegetation. On one walk which I made in mid-summer with a group of mentally handicapped young adults we identified well over a hundred different flowering plants on a path around the cliff tops. It is easy to generate enthusiasm for collecting and searching, and even the most ardent city-dweller can become excited by finding a new flower for the list. Butterflies, beetles and other insects can also be noticed in the search for flowers. Small and common blue butterflies flit among the yellow vetches and trefoils on which their caterpillars feed. Large red admirals and painted ladies, both of which migrate here from N. Africa, tortoiseshells and peacocks are all common on a hot sunny day, especially towards the end of summer. The common brown butterflies – grayling, wall, meadow brown and ringlet, the more brightly patterned species of fritillary, clouded yellows and small coppers – are easy to identify with the aid of a simple field guide, and some patience to watch them.

Sand dunes

Our large dune systems often border the mouths of river estuaries, and while we can view them by car from a distance it is really necessary to take to a path and explore these wild places on foot. Dunes form behind a sandy beach, especially when sand accumulates against cliffs or in a small valley. Golf courses often are made in established dune systems and give possible access by road and tracks. A mini desert is created in the midst of an extensive line of dunes, as the sand swirls in the wind and plants strive to survive in a hostile environment. As in deserts, water is at a premium, and plants have special adaptations for survival. Most abundant are the grasses, notably the dense tussocks of sharp pointed leaves of marram grass. Each leaf is rolled and grooved to reduce the surface for water loss. Airpores are sunk into the grooves and the leaf surface is waxy. Roots and underground stems probe deep into the sand in search of water, in turn anchoring the plant against moving sand and thus stabilising the dunes. Other grasses are able to survive occasional submergence in seawater at spring tides, and can grow at the edge of the drift line and dunes. The sea couch grass resembles the garden weed, with long runners beneath the sand surface from which rise small narrow leaves. The sea lyme grass is tall and has broad-bladed, blue-green leaves, often with a yellow spike of flowers resembling a cereal crop. These grasses form obstacles to the wind carrying sand from the beach, and the sand is deposited on the leeward side to fall initially into small hummocks and ultimately high dune hills.

As the sand becomes more stable further plants can grow: mosses carpet the surface and hold in moisture for small seedlings to grow. Some inland plants survive – speedwell, scarlet pimpernel, birds foot trefoil, ragwort, groundsel, yellow bedstraw. Typical of dunes are the dramatic sea holly, with prickly waxy leaves and pale blue flowers seen in August; sea bindweed, rooting deeply into the sand, with large, pink trumpet-shaped flowers; yellow horned poppy, with hairy leaves to which water drops cling, keeping the plant moist. More sand is held down by the creeping sand sedge, which appears to grow in straight lines, several green shoots growing at regular intervals from a long underground stem.

On large dunes the landward regions become so stable as to be indistinguishable from pastureland or heathland. Rabbits often abound on dunes and dune grassland, creating erosion by their burrowing activity. Man also erodes dunes by trampling vegetation, parking cars or even sun-bathing in the warmth and protection of sand hills. Certain areas are consequently often fenced off for conservation programmes, by planting marram grass and encouraging sand to settle.

While dune plants may be obvious, animal life is rarely easy to detect. This is because animals must search shelter away from the drying effects of wind and sun, often among the dense grass tussocks. But shrews and field mice come out to feed at night, and on a few dunes the rare natterjack toad can be heard noisily croaking. Mostly it is insects and spiders that can be seen by day, by peering into a clump of marram grass among the moist dead

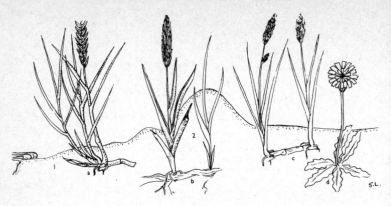

Fig. 7.10   Dune plant life: a. sea couch grass   b. marram
grass   c. sand sedge   d. hawksbit   e. birdsfoot trefoil   f.
marsh orchid   g. helliborine   h. brown bent grass   i. sea
buckthorn (1. Embryo dunes   2. Foredunes   3. Dune
slack   4. Fixed dune   5. Dune scrub)

leaf litter. The sand surface may be scattered with shells of the
banded snail, *Cepaea*: yellow, pink and brown shells, banded
with varying patterns of brown markings. Collect these shells
and examine them to see the variation within the single species.
Find an 'anvil' stone where gulls and other birds have opened
them and note the colour of the broken shell fragments. The
shell colour and pattern camouflages the snail against bird
predators, and the shell remains will be those more easily seen by
the gulls.

Lie on the sand among the dune hills and observe how much
warmer and less windy it becomes; dig your hand deep into the
sand and see how cool and damp it feels compared with the hot,
dry surface; creep into a dense marram tussock and smell the
mouldy accumulation of rotting leaf litter with creeping beetles,
woodlice, millipedes and spiders. There is much to be taught by
nature in this environment and much to learn.

Estuaries and salt marsh
In sheltered bays and creeks and the mouths of large rivers there
are areas where the sea deposits mud, and at low tide extensive
mudflats or 'saltings' form the feeding grounds for a variety of

wading birds. The long bills of curlews, godwits and oystercat-
chers probe deep into the mud for small molluscs and crustaceans. Dunlin, redshank and greenshank move about feeding
at the edge of the water in deeper channels, occasionally flying
in rapid zig-zag movements at some disturbance. In winter
migrant brent geese feed on the beds of eel grass on east coast
flats and marshes, while further north flocks of greylag and
pinkfoot, barnacle and whitefront geese descend from Arctic
breeding grounds to the Solway, Tay and Tees. Bird sanctuaries
and reserves have been established on many coastal estuaries,
notably at Slimbridge on the Severn where the Wildfowl Trust
have their own visiting centre with hides overlooking the
mudflats and shoreline. Wetlands are at a premium in modern
day society, since so many are lost by drainage for farming or
industrial developments, and consequently many have been
bought by the Royal Society for the Protection of Birds as
Nature Reserves. Some near the coast are suitable for wheelchair access, in particular at Minsmere on the Suffolk coast,
where avocets breed annually on man-made scrapes and can be
observed from hides built with wheelchairs in mind. Details of
these reserves can be obtained from the R.S.P.B.

There are also many places where disabled birdwatchers can
get close to estuaries, mudflats, reedbeds and shorelines from the
road. Consult the local O.S. maps and see where roads meet the
sea and rivermouth. By trial and error you will discover a
number of suitable observation points.

The plants of both estuary and salt marsh are adapted to salt-water flooding at high tides and regular deposits of silt and mud. Most common on the mud at the water edge is glasswort or

Fig. 7.11 Salt marsh plants: a. glasswort b. sea purslane c. sea thrift d. sea lavender (1. Estuary 2. Mudflats 3. Creek 4. Salt pan)

marsh samphire, a succulent-leaved annual which germinates each year. The short stem is formed from a number of jointed segments which carry no proper leaves. There are large expanses of bare mud between the occasional green clump of glasswort, but as one moves landward the vegetation becomes more dense. Seablite, sea aster and sea lavender give colour to the marsh, and a sheet of mauve sea lavender in late summer is a glorious sight. Smaller plants of sea spurrey and white scurvy grass grow among the shrubby bushes of sea purslane, which often forms a characteristic sward along the margins of creeks. It appears to require the better drainage of the banks: as the tide swirls in along the creeks it deposits mud among the roots and stems of the purslane shrubs, so eventually raising the level of the mudflats above that of the incoming tide, until the marsh begins to dry out. As it becomes better drained the purslane grows more luxuriantly until it swamps all other vegetation.

Small shallow pools, or 'pans', are often left above the general level of high tide, where the salinity of the water can rise or fall with sun and rain. Animals inhabiting these salt pans must be able to tolerate such wide fluctuations of conditions and small species of shrimp-like crustacea (*Gammarus*) and crabs are among the few inhabitants. Glasswort too can grow under such conditions since it is the most salt-adapted plant on the marsh. Without grazing, reeds will completely cover flat coastal areas above a certain tidal level, especially where freshwater enters the salt marsh. This gradual transition to swamp heralds the arrival of a variety of freshwater marsh plants and forms a new community ideal for the breeding reed and sedge warblers, rails and bittern. For the naturalist the coastal scene offers great variety and the handicapped person can derive much pleasure from it.

8.   MOOR AND MOUNTAIN

Introduction

Highland scenery

Rocks and minerals

Moulding the landscape

Heath, moor and bog

Mountain life – the montane zone

Remains of prehistoric man

Exploring the hills

Exploration planning

Camping

Expeditions

8. MOOR AND MOUNTAIN

Introduction
Access to open countryside is important for the disabled
person, but much of our more exciting landscape is in hilly
moorland districts. Our National Parks and Nature Reserves,
notable areas of wildlife and remoteness, should be there for
everyone, whether handicapped or able-bodied, so we discuss
how handicapped people can be offered access to more remote
areas. In this chapter we look first at how the British landscape
has been moulded, at the rocks and minerals we might find, and
then describe how to make a collection. The plants and animals
of heaths, moors and mountains can be of great interest to the
disabled naturalist – a land of deer, eagles and rare plants. We
learn a little of man's origins and the relics of his past: stone
circles and tombs, hill forts and mounds. The hills are exciting to
explore and we see that the disabled can be provided for in
camps, treks and expeditions.

Highland scenery
Wild and desolate, wind-swept and wet describe much of the
British landscape, for wherever we live we are not too far away
from high ground. Scotland and Wales especially are regions of
moor and mountain, but much of the west and north of England
has similar scenery. If we look at a map of the British Isles we will
notice that highland terrain exists west of a line drawn from the
central Peak District. Many such regions now have been
designated as National Parks, where outdoor activities can take
place amidst a carefully protected environment. Farming and
forestry still continue within the Parks, but building and
industry, notably mining activities, are mainly forbidden.
Although the National Parks Commission was established in
1949 they are now the responsibility of the Countryside
Commission, which is currently examining access for the

disabled in wild places. In England the principal National Parks occur in Northumberland, the North Yorkshire Moors and Yorkshire Dales, the Lake District and Peak District, Exmoor and Dartmoor, while in Wales both Snowdonia and the Brecon Beacons enjoy this protection. Many other remote highland areas have been declared National Nature Reserves under the protection of the Nature Conservancy, a notable example being the Cairngorms in the Scottish Highlands. The Royal Society for the Protection of Birds and many local Conservation Trusts have also established reserves in similar locations. Much of our wild heritage is thus protected from developments which would spoil and detract from the natural beauty of the landscape. Countryside is there to walk and hike in, trek and camp in. Moors and mountains are marvellous places for a country holiday.

In the British Isles mountains are usually regarded as land which rises above 600 metres (2000 feet) although if you mark on your map the land at an altitude over 1000 metres you will see it is mainly restricted to Scotland, although peaks in Snowdonia and the Lake District will also be included. Our highest mountain is Ben Nevis (1343 m.). The Scottish Highlands are composed of hard rocks which have eroded slowly over millions of years. The study of rocks and minerals is called *geology*, and it is possible to construct a geological map of Britain to see which rocks form our major mountain districts.

Rocks and minerals

Our oldest rocks are *igneous* in nature, having been formed millions of years ago in Pre-Cambrian times by the cooling of molten material. Red-hot liquid rocks flowed from volcanoes and cracks in the earth, and although our nearest active volcanoes are now in Iceland, once upon a time much of Britain was formed in this manner. When such liquid rock cooled at the earth's surface (*extrusive*) it formed volcanic rock, including *basalt*. The mountains of the Lake District had a volcanic origin. But not all hard igneous rocks formed this way. Some are large masses of molten rocks which forced their way deep down between other rocks (*intrusive*), and cooled slowly to form *plutonic* rocks, notably *granite*. Volcanic rocks are named after Vulcan, the Roman God of Fire, while Plutonic rocks gain their name

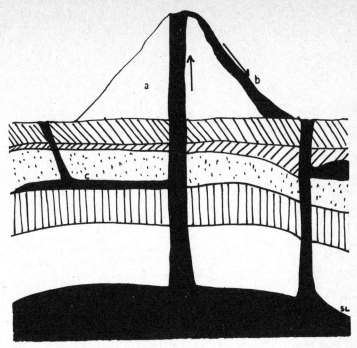

Fig. 8.1 Formation of igneous rocks: a. volcano b. lava forms volcanic rock (basalt) c. formation of plutonic rock (granite)

from Pluto, the Roman God of the Underworld. The major granite regions of England are in the south-west counties, Cornwall and Devon, where granite *tors* typify the scenery of Bodmin Moor and Dartmoor. In Scotland the large Cairngorm plateau and much of our highest mountain, Ben Nevis, are similarly found to be formed of granite. In Northumberland the famous Roman Wall built by Emperor Hadrian stands on top of Whin Sill; such sills being bands of igneous rock forced between layers of other rocks. The softer rocks above were gradually worn away by the forces of erosion, leaving behind a horizontal band of hard rock standing above the ground. Liquid igneous rocks were made of many minerals, and granite regions are especially rich in metals and have been mined since man discovered the use of iron, copper and tin. When these rocks cooled minerals formed different crystals, especially *quartz*, a very hard mineral. Amethyst and citrine are two forms of quartz, both semi-precious stones.

During the early history of the earth the rocks were gradually worn away by the action of ice, notably glaciers, and water. Mountain streams and rivers gradually erode rocks and deposit sediments at sea. Under great pressure these sediments ultimately turn into rock: muds and silts become clay, sands form sandstone and even pebbles cement together to produce a *conglomerate*. These are all *sedimentary* rocks. But not all sedimentary rocks form from surface rock washed into the sea. Some

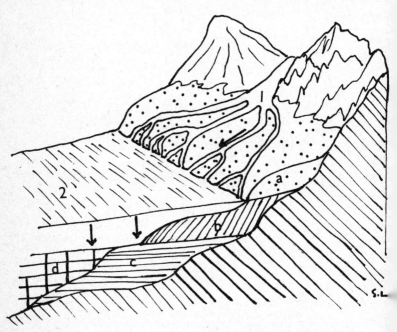

Fig. 8.2 Formation of sedimentary rocks: a. conglomerate b. sandstone c. clay d. limestone (1. river 2. sea)

rocks are produced from the sediments of living organisms (*organic sediments*). Shells of marine life settled on the sea bed and under pressure from above became limestone and chalk. Fossils of these animals can still be found in such rocks. Limestone formations represent much older rocks than the more recent chalk of south and east England. Plants under pressure in the Carboniferous period formed our coal deposits, notably in South Wales, central and north-east England. Sedimentary rocks were pushed above sea level by enormous forces in the earth's crust, from below or the side, which caused mountains to arch upwards as a series of folds. In this way the major world mountains were formed; the Alps, Pyrenees, Himalayas, Rockies and Andes. Some ranges such as the Alps are still upfolding today at about 1mm. each year. In Britain the Pennines arose as a large limestone mass which has eroded to create the characteristic scenery of the Peaks, Dales and Fells. Great heat and pressure can change rocks, not only soft sedimentary materials but also hard igneous rocks. As molten rock rises, surrounding rocks become transformed by the heat, and in this manner limestone changes into marble. During the changes in pressure due to folding, clays become pressed into slate and soft coal into anthracite. Rocks, produced by such a change from existing rocks, are called *metamorphic*. Much of the Scottish Highlands is metamorphic in origin, mainly *schist*, formed from transformed siltstone and mudstone (fine sedimentary materials) and *gneiss*, formed from the igneous granite.

Collecting rocks and minerals is an interesting and worthwhile hobby. All children like to bring home some stones from a visit to the coast, river or mountain and there are many good books to help in identification. Eventually you may want a geology hammer, but in the first instance you can collect many specimens and learn much about rocks by collecting stones or splitting pieces with a heavy hammer and chisel. Take care when hitting rocks, because small pieces may easily hurt the eyes. Rocks and minerals can be stored in separate boxes, or placed in a cabinet when the collection grows. Each specimen should be labelled with a small, self-adhesive label noting type of rock and the location where it was found.

Moulding the landscape

During millions of years the rocks we have just examined have been moulded into a landscape by the actions of weather and forces of erosion. The landscape in different parts of Britain offers stark contrasts: the flatter rolling lands of the South Downs are very different from the jutting peaks of North Wales, and the dissected limestone scenery of the Pennines is completely different from the exposed granite rocky tors on Dartmoor.

The major actions of weathering have occurred by extreme changes in temperature on the rocks. Water seeps into cracks and fissures, freezes then turns to ice. During this process it expands, forcing the rocks further apart. When ice thaws again small pieces, or even large pieces, of rock break away to form the characteristic *scree* slopes of rock debris on sides and at the foot of the mountain. In limestone districts rain falling on to the softer rock is of a weakly acid nature, due to carbon dioxide in the air dissolving in the rain. The acidic water wears away the rock by chemical action. You can test this at home by dropping a piece of chalk or limestone rock into vinegar, also a weak acid. It froths and fizzes and may eventually be completely dissolved. Joints between slabs of limestone in the Pennines have become wide gaps, over a long period of time, forming the characteristic limestone pavement scenery such as can be seen on the high Yorkshire Dales.

We must not forget that plant roots too, growing down between the rocks, can cause them to split apart, where they may be further weathered by frost or chemical action. But Britain's mountains have been mainly sculptured by the action of ice, and in the history of our Isles much of northern Britain has at some time been covered by immense glaciers reaching down from Arctic Regions. A glacier is ice which has accumulated in a valley, and it moves slowly from high to low ground, eroding the

Fig. 8.3   Mountains and glaciers: a. glacier   b. moraine

sides and floor of the valley as it passes. Rock debris accumulates in front and beneath the glacier, and when eventually the glacier retreats as temperatures rise this rock remains where it was deposited to form a *moraine*. Sometimes large boulders are moved over vast distances in this manner, and are left in unusual situations where they are called *erratics*. In Snowdonia the famous Llanberis Pass, through which you can hike or drive in the car, was formed as a glaciated valley. Take the mountain railway to the summit of Snowdon and you will pass through an

Fig. 8.4 A glaciated valley

area once covered with a great ice sheet. The scenery is typical of that shaped by the action of glaciers during the Ice Ages. Mount Snowdon itself was formed by a number of glaciers which began in large ice-filled basins (the *corrie* or *cwm*). The summit represents the higher land between the corries which was not covered by ice. Look at a map of that part of North Wales and see how many features bear the name *cwm*. Today, many such hollows are filled with water, making a small lake (*Llyn*) surrounded by high mountainous land.

Rivers too, have played a significant role in the development of our landscape. Water erodes the rocks over which it flows, eating into the banks to form valleys and washing debris towards the sea. We have already seen that rivers may arise from surface rainfall producing small streams, or rise from underground as springs. In limestone districts erosion of rock by underground water has produced caves, and the subsequent collapse of such caverns may form a *gorge*, such as Gordale Scar, near Malham, in the north Pennines, and the famous Cheddar Gorge in the Mendip Hills of Somerset, our nearest approach to a canyon. You can visit the caves at Cheddar and see many of the underground features of limestone scenery. The Clifton Gorge, near Bristol, was the result of powerful water action by the River Avon, wearing through an outcrop of Carboniferous limestone and leaving almost vertical valley sides. Today we can still see the role played by water as an erosion force by examining the granite Dartmoor *tors*. Much of this desolate

Fig. 8.5　A granite tor

ground features exposed slabs of hard rock, transformed into weird shapes, the result of very slow wearing away of the granite along horizontal and vertical joints. Rain passing down between such joints is still carving new rock features. The *Tor* is a large mass of granite which has so far resisted complete disintegration.

Look at your map of Devon and Cornwall and see how many place-names feature the word *tor*.

The story of our landscape is a long one; a story of fire and ice, hard and soft rocks, rivers and rain, but a story full of interest. Look around when next you travel in the car or train to other parts of the country, and imagine how it all must have looked through the long periods of change.

Heath, moor and bog

While much of upland Britain is covered in remote moorland, there are vast tracts of lowland country in south and east England which appear similar and may be termed heathland. The principal areas of heath occur in Hampshire (the New Forest area), in the London basin, in the Breckland of East Anglia and in more isolated areas such as the Lizard Peninsula at the far west of Cornwall. They were cleared of native woodland in early times to create more areas for grazing and were periodically burned to destroy old, woody vegetation and encourage young shoots of plants. Many heaths are no longer grazed or burned, but fire still poses a major threat to heathland habitat. The soil in these areas is mostly poor and acid, although this is untrue on the Lizard where the *serpentine* rocks produce local areas of high nutrient status, permitting the growth of particular species. Heathers and ling dominate the scene, providing a purple carpet in late summer and autumn. Ling in particular will form dense shrub growth over 15–20 years, with thick but straggling woody stems, restricting light from reaching the lower ground layer plants. Dead leaves fall to provide a humus layer to the impoverished soil. The products of humus decomposition are washed-out (*leached*) by rain forming a typical soil profile (*podsol*) similar to that found in conifer woodlands. Unmanaged heaths often have dense stands of ling, surrounded by more delicate heathers, notably bell-heather and cross-leaved heath. The former prefers well drained soils, while the latter grows best on wet heathland. The acid nature of the soil encourages plants which grow well where there is no lime in the soil (*calcifuge plants*), such as the yellow tormentil and pale blue milkwort. Gorse is especially common on our heaths, providing ideal nesting habitat for the rare Dartford Warbler now restricted to only a few localities in southern England.

While gorse may flower over most of the year, much of the yellow colour mixing with the autumn purple carpet of heather is formed by Western Gorse. This smaller, more prostrate species is to be found on the heaths west of Poole, in Dorset, and provides for much beauty on the coastal heaths of Cornwall. A flowering parasitic plant, dodder, can be found on the roots of gorse and heather, and on wet heathland typical moor and bog plants occur.

Heathland communities are noted for the presence of particular animals, but it is the reptiles which are especially well represented. All six British species occur in this habitat, with the smooth snake and sand lizard almost entirely restricted to a few southern heaths. Grass snakes and adder, slow-worms and the viviparous lizard are more widespread in their distribution. Large areas of bracken fern often harbour heathland butterflies like the green hairstreak, silver-studded blue and grayling – the Cornish coastal footpath around Lands End will yield all three species in mid-summer.

Moors typically cover large areas of upland in the north and west, characterised by high rainfall and poor, shallow, acid soils. No trees grow, for the soil has no depth and the wind is too extreme, so on many moors grasses form the dominant plant cover. The principal moorland shrubs of the Scottish Highlands are heathers and ling, although the purple fruits of bilberry are to be found on damp peat soils and cowberry, crowberry and bearberry all occur under various conditions on our moors. Where grazing and burning have destroyed the heather, a grass moor develops: bent and fescue on dry, fertile soils, wavy-hair grass on dry, poor soils; and mat-grass, purple moor-grass and deer-sedge on wet, acid peat soils. Water accumulates in pockets, creating waterlogged conditions and encouraging growth of bog plants. In such circumstances peat deposits form in the soil, producing even more acid conditions.

Bogs arise wherever drainage is poor and there is no lime in the soil to neutralise the acid. There are three types of bog – *valley*, *raised* and *blanket*. Valley bogs form in shallow depressions and can be found on the southern heaths. Bog moss (*Sphagnum*) dominates the scene, and holds considerable quantities of acid water in the large cells of the leaves. Peat is formed from bog moss under these conditions. Typical bog plants colonise such

Fig. 8.6   Some moorland plants: a. bell heather   b. ling   c. cross-leaved heath   d. bilberry   e. sundew

habitats – marsh cinquefoil, bog myrtle and sundew. Round leaves, covered with bright red hairs, identify this last, insect-eating plant. Each hair has a small sticky 'blob' at the tip, and insects attracted to the bright leaves of sundew soon become entangled on the leaf surface. Gradually the insect body is digested by juices released from the leaf and all soluble products are absorbed by the plant to supplement the natural nutrient deficiency of the soil.

Raised bogs develop where rainfall is very high, on top of valley bogs, by the continued growth of bog moss. Some form above streams, or even a small lake, and produce a 'quaking bog' such as may be found on Dartmoor. It is dangerous for animals to walk on such a bog since they can sink through the moss peat cover and disappear into a lower watery grave. Much of central Ireland is covered with raised bog, which continues to grow upwards, eventually forming a dome. The bog 'surface breaks into pools and hummocks, the latter gradually drying out and eventually becoming dominated by heather. Different species of bog moss colonise the pools, with dryer hummocks and other species in between. The various colours of vegetation – red, yellow, green – produce a patchwork across the surface of the bog.

Blanket bogs form when bog moss continues to cover the land under high rainfall conditions. Many of our mountainous districts are carpets of blanket bog – the Pennines, Wales, Dartmoor. Rannoch Moor in the Scottish Highlands too is an area of blanket bog, with plants such as cotton grass, deer sedge and butterwort, another insectivorous species.

Many wet moorlands have recently been drained to allow forestry development; and peat-digging, especially in Ireland and Scotland, has always been a form of moorland management. Peat was removed for household fuel on a regular cyclic pattern, allowing further accumulation of this black layer in subsequent years. However, without doubt the most important factor in the development of our moorland scene has been close grazing by sheep. Huge areas of upland grassland have been farmed in this manner for several hundred years. Although the grazing is often poor the land has been cheap to purchase. Only certain breeds are able to tolerate the harsh climate of the upper moors, and their tracks make the easiest paths to follow across the desolate landscape. Sheep tend to graze certain grasses such as bent and fescue and leave others, and this fact has led to the spread of the mat grass.

Red deer formerly lived in the dense forests of pine, especially in the Scottish hills, but as timber was removed this large animal was forced on to the open moorlands, notably in the Highland regions. Now they roam and graze the high tops of the Cairngorms and Angus glens, descending only in winter when snow conditions prohibit feeding. At that time they may enter forestry plantations causing damage to young trees and necessitating restriction of the population. In winter, white mountain hares burrow among the snow in search of lush plant shoots and fall prey to both birds and mammal predators. Stoats, which also turn white in the Scottish winter, when they are known as ermine, and weasels are typical of the smaller carnivores, but it is the wild cat that we most associate with the remote highland terrain. Birds of prey are typical of this environment: eagles, buzzard, harrier and peregrine, all search among the moors and mountains for an unsuspecting lamb or hare. Merlin hunt the moors, taking smaller birds whilst still in flight. The moorland heather carpet is home for the grouse and ptarmigan, both birds spending their whole year in the uplands. Others visit the moor only to nest – curlew, golden plover and dunlin – and depart for the coast in winter months. Migrating wheatear and whinchat mix with resident pipits and larks, and so the moor has bird-life for all seasons.

Mountain life – the montane zone

In the large mountain ranges of other lands the true montane zone does not begin until great altitudes are reached. In the Alps this is at about 2500 metres, but in this country our mountains are smaller and the true mountain life appears at less than 1000 metres. At this height, above the tree-line, a harsh climate prevails and wildlife must be hardy and adaptable. Poor, shallow soils and exposed rock surfaces mean that mountain plants must seek shelter and protection in narrow cracks and fissures in the mountain side, under overhanging rocks or by the side of a moss-covered stream. Water flowing down the mountain washes out valuable nutrients from the underlying rocks, thus encouraging plants to colonise the wet, rich *flushes* that are created. Rare orchids grow alongside the insectivorous plants, finding good rooting conditions in the wet green carpet. Arctic-Alpine plants, relics of an earlier Ice Age, cling to an often precarious existence among the rocks and crags, creating an illusion of far-away landscapes. Most montane plants cannot tolerate competition with other species and therefore grow alone, isolated in a bare environment. Many require a lime-rich soil and are to be found in mountains where limestone outcrops occur. Several areas are famous for their plant life: Ben Lawers in Perthshire is a particularly well known nature reserve where plants more typical of Greenland, Iceland, Scandinavia and the Alps may grow. Alpine gentian, with delicate blue flowers, alpine forget-me-not and rare saxifrages, more often seen in the rock garden at home, are all encountered and protected. Other Arctic-Alpines have a wider distribution on our mountains. Alpine Lady's mantle, mountain avens, starry saxifrage, mossy saxifrage and the succulent roseroot may be seen in the mountains of Snowdonia as well as in the Highlands of Scotland. The mountain flora in Britain consists of about 130 species, although few of us will have the opportunity to see many of them.

Only three birds breed in the montane zone – the ptarmigan, snow bunting and dotterel. Ptarmigan, like many arctic species of birds and mammals, turns white in winter, forming good camouflage against a snowy background. In summer it is mottled brown-grey above and is again difficult to see among rocks and lichens. Like the grouse, ptarmigans do not fly far, but in autumn they flock into coveys which may move to lower ground. Ptarmigan feed on shoots of mountain shrubs such as bilberry and crowberry, and heather. Snow bunting and dotterel are both naturally arctic birds, breeding in latitudes far north. Snow buntings nest commonly in Greenland, Iceland and Scandinavia, their black and white plumage in that environment rather more vivid than the brown and white pattern we see on the birds when they visit us in winter. A few pairs remain to nest on the high plateau of the Cairngorms, in the Scottish Highlands, and it is the same locality where we must look for nesting dotterel. This species too has a dramatic breeding plumage, the grey chest and russet flanks contrasting with a brown back and black head. In addition a white stripe through the eye makes this bird easy to identify. Dotterel, a relative of the plovers, breed mainly in northern Scandinavia, but are to be seen in Britain while migrating to and from Africa. Certain places tend to attract such migrant birds each year. The dotterel is unusual in that the male incubates the eggs and the female is dominant in the display. They are also very tame birds and may be approached both when on the nest and when seen during migrations.

Although mountain regions may become places for visiting summer butterflies, there is only one alpine species in Britain – the mountain ringlet. This dark brown, almost black species, appears in the Lake District and central Scotland, the caterpillar feeding on mat grass. Other insects living at high altitude include a variety of beetles, some attractive in colour, and the interesting black, wingless snow-fly (*Boreus*) which can be found in winter on snow beds. Related to scorpion flies, the small larvae and adults feed on moss leaves.

Few mammals live naturally on our mountain tops, but the minute pygmy shrew, the smallest British species – only about 6omm (2½ inches) long – will ascend even our highest mountain (1343 m. on Ben Nevis). The mountain hare has been found from 330 m. to 1300 m., but is not common above 800 m. in the montane zone. Like that of its predator, the stoat, which also ascends mountains, the fur turns white in winter so that both hunter and hunted are masked against a snowy background.

Remains of Prehistoric Man

The Highland zone of Britain was colonised in very early times by successive human cultures, each of which has left behind a wide array of antiquities. Remote and exposed moorlands from Cornwall to Shetland yield evidence of settlement by our ancestors; huts and farms, stone circles and henges, tombs and barrows. Huge stone monuments stand erect against a flat expanse of peat, bog and heather moor, many having remained thus for some five thousand years. Although early settlement has usually been from the south and east, our lowland region, man has spread north and west towards our mountains and hills, often driven further by new waves of more successful cultures.

During the Early stone age (*Palaeolithic*), climatic conditions largely limited man to the Thames basin, since this was an era of glaciations. Later he was able to spread north to the Yorkshire Dales and west into regions of Wales. *Mesolithic* man, about ten thousand years ago, dwelt on open moors and heaths in southern England, the south Pennines and north York moors. But it was during the New Stone age (*Neolithic*) that man constructed the large megalithic tombs typical of moorland landscapes. Such masons entered Britain from the south-west and settled the lands of Cornwall, around the Bristol Channel, south-west Scotland, Aberdeenshire and Orkney. They were our first farmers, fashioning tools from local stone and establishing a living pattern from which modern civilisation was built. Examples of their stone *megaliths* are found in the eastern Mediterranean, so their skills may have been brought west into much of Europe and eventually to Britain by metal prospectors, farmers or missionaries. These burial tombs were collective, and after each burial the tomb was closed and ritually sealed. About two thousand megaliths survive today in all regions of Britain, but essentially in the Highland zone. New Stone Age burial mounds, or *barrows*, are also seen in lowland regions, notably as

Fig. 8.7   Remains of ancient man: a. quoit   b. megalithic tomb   c. stone circle

mounds of earth or chalk on the downland scene. Dorset, Sussex and Wiltshire are the best areas for seeing long barrows, although by far the most numerous of such antiquities are the round barrows of the later Bronze Age. The early *Beaker* people arrived from the Rhine area about four thousand years ago, introducing the use of copper for tools and weapons. It was this culture that developed the idea of *henge* monuments, fashioning the famous constructions at Stonehenge and Avebury on the chalk downs of Wiltshire. The mineral rich landscapes of Cornwall and Wales were later colonised by Bronze Age man, providing vital metals for development of his crafts. It was only a matter of time before the new metal, iron, was introduced to Britain by three waves of settlers from mainland Europe and the great Iron Age arrived. Iron became cheaper, and ore was plentiful. Tools and weapons evolved and by the time of the Roman invasions the tools of Iron Age man very closely resembled those of today.

Single, standing stones, or *monoliths*, are more often encountered than the more complex henge. Erected as monuments in the late Stone and Bronze Ages, they can be seen on high ground, on moors and in fields. Some were grouped as three or five stones, to produce a *dolmen*, a capstone set on top to make the tomb. The entire stone structure was covered with earth, but time has eroded this covering leaving behind only a cluster of rock. Many *cairns*, or piles of stones, marking routes on the exposed uplands of the Pennine Way, date from Bronze and Iron Ages, and mark prehistoric burial sites.

Knowing more about our origins often makes travel through desolate landscapes all the more interesting. Take your camera or sketch book and visit some of our antiquities. Find out about these stone remains: many are official Ancient Monuments and can be found marked on the local O.S. map. Guide books and leaflets to the more popular sites are often available and there is a good field guide to assist in the identification and interpretation of these links with our past.

Exploring the hills

All young people want to explore: to seek new things and new places and to undertake new experiences. The handicapped youngster should have the same opportunity as others to develop this inquisitive instinct and to develop skills which might otherwise pass him by. Exploration develops curiosity, confidence, leadership and determination – all skills which play a significant role in our total social development. Hiking across a rough tract of moorland, negotiating a stile, crossing a stream, or camping on an isolated mountainside may appear to have little direct relevance to life in the city centre, but this is far from the truth. Out-of-door experiences are an integral part of our total development and should not be neglected.

Hiking and trekking with physically able, but mentally handicapped children, adolescents and young adults, is a great experience, and fairly easy to organise. For those confined to a wheelchair, or with other problems of mobility, access becomes much more critical and exploration may be more limited in extent, but not in importance. Many handicapped young people can learn to ride horses and ponies at home or through school, perhaps with a local Riding for the Disabled Centre. In moorland or hilly districts such as Dartmoor, North Wales, the Brecons and the Pennines there are numerous centres for pony trekking, even for those confined to wheelchairs. Forest 'walks' in moorland and hilly districts often have good road surfaces for vehicle access by local workers. Even in the Highlands of Scotland there are many excellent routes into the glens which are well maintained for winter sports enthusiasts; and normal road systems in the Pennines, North Wales, Dartmoor and Bodmin Moor lead direct on to the open moors. A successful trek for the wheelchair user needs to be both shorter than for the able bodied and easier in the going, but provided that the landscape is exciting and the route made more interesting by knowledge of the local area, this can be just as successful as a climb to Snowdon itself. I have often found sufficient to stimulate and excite the minds of young handicapped persons in only a few hundred yards of moorland terrain. Look at the rocks and landscape, at flowers and birds, at relics of the past; imagine how early people lived there, how they ate and farmed the land. Taste the water, look at the soil and feel the atmosphere of the environment. With one small group of adolescents we were even able to build ourselves a stone-age style hut circle on the exposed moorland, and imagine ourselves as part of that distant past.

Exploration planning

Preparation should be as much a part of the total exercise as actually going on a trek. First decide on your area and plan the route according to your access requirements and limitations.

Study the local O.S. map (1:50,000) and learn to read all the information a map can provide. First, what is the scale? How far is it from point to point? You may not be able to follow a direct route, because a river, mountain or other natural obstacle may be in the way. How far is the detour? Take a length of string and place it accurately along your actual route. Mark the end-point on your string (a felt-tip pen is suitable) and then place the string on the scale-line given on the map, to calculate the total distance in miles (or km.). Look for landmarks on the map – old monuments, water courses, a remote farm and the shape of the land as revealed by the map contours. These can tell you about the gradient of slope up a hill or down a valley, since the closer the contour lines are together the greater will be the gradient. Try making a relief model with flat polystyrene (ceiling tiles) cut to shape and fixed in layers with a suitable adhesive. If map reading is too difficult for your group to interpret, then try taking some photographs of the route before you depart and use these rather than a map and compass. Different land forms and landmarks can thus be visually identified if the pictures are taken on the trek. The leader should feel confident about reading a map and compass, which must always accompany the group even if others will not be using them. The map can be kept on a clip board under polythene or in a proper map-bag, where it is dry and easy to read. In planning the route allow ample time for slow walkers (or 'pushers'), rough terrain, frequent stops for drinks and food and time for examining the area. Remember, a good short hike which everyone enjoys is better than a long, arduous trek which only you can manage.

Before your actual departure find out about the weather in that district. There may be local variations, especially in mountain regions, so try to obtain a weather report from some authority living in the place to be visited. Coastguards, stations belonging to the Armed Forces and the Police are all bodies that can be approached. Remember to inform some authority that you are going on your trek and perhaps leave details of your planned route and expected times of departure and return. It is easier to avoid difficulties in rescue, when needed, if there is adequate information supplied in advance.

What to take and wear – in addition to the map and compass there are a number of essential items for the rucsac. A good first aid kit is a must, and someone should preferably have a good working knowledge of first aid. Assemble the kit with care and check it regularly to re-stock items. The most frequent accidents are minor and can be dealt with easily if you have what is needed at the time. Sunburn, insect stings, grazed knees and cut fingers are typical happenings when out of doors. Your local St. John Ambulance Centre will help in providing instruction and in planning your first aid kit. In addition, some other items are useful to carry with you:

Penknife	Matches (in waterproof bag)
Scissors	Torch
Pencil	Sticky tape
Notebook	Coins (for telephone)
Whistle	Safety pins
String	Glucose sweets

You can design your own emergency supply kit packed tightly into a polythene box, within a polythene bag. In heavy rain your rucsac may well leak to some extent, so put all the contents inside a large polythene bag first.

Your food on a one-day hike will usually be prepared in advance, rather than cooked on site, but ensure that you take some spare rations and emergency supplies. Chocolate, nuts, raisins, are high in energy content and good to eat, raising both your body temperature and your spirits. Keep this emergency food for its real purpose – it is better to bring it back home with you than to eat it too early! A drink for everyone will also be necessary. Clothing needs to be weatherproof and warm, but not too heavy and restricting movement. Remember, the person confined to a wheelchair cannot generate his/her own heat, and will need to be well protected from the cold, especially in the legs. Wear a hat in hot and cold weather, since it keeps you warm and prevents sunstroke. Take gloves – cold hands become quite painful, especially when wet. A good anorak is better than a woollen coat, which becomes wet and heavy in rain. A nylon cagoule can provide your waterproof layer and is light to carry. Warmth is best supplied by several layers of thin clothes rather than by one, heavy sweater. You can always peel off single layers when you get too warm. Your legs are best covered in cord trousers rather than jeans, which tend to soak up water and become uncomfortable. Girls should always wear trousers and the leader should check that everyone is well-clothed before departing on the trek.

Footwear can be a problem. Heavy socks or several pairs of normal grade socks will keep your feet warm. While proper hiking or climbing boots are undoubtedly best, few will own them, and others may not be able to wear them. Most walkers can produce wellington boots, but many who are ambulent but handicapped have walking problems and cannot wear wellingtons. Generally speaking good tough shoes are best under these circumstances, with plenty of water repellant rubbed into the tops and seams to keep the feet dry. When hiking, your feet become the most important part of the body, so take care of them. Plasters on sore places are better than blisters, but if someone suffers from this problem return immediately rather than trek on and cause great discomfort.

Finally decide on some project work or topics for observation and collection during the hike. Anything can become more interesting than walking along in silence, and distances quickly pass when you are busy looking for plants, birds or butterflies. Take whatever you need to record observations (camera, spare films, notebook, art pad, pencil, crayons, or felt pens). Sketching and photography on the hike is more fun than the school art class! Take polythene bags and plastic boxes to collect plants: leaves, flowers, mosses and lichens. Small stones and pieces of rock can be put in a lunch box to bring home. A pair of binoculars greatly enhances your day out, since you can identify birds and even watch a grazing herd of deer. Encourage everyone to be involved, and try to keep your group together as a single party, rather than a long, straggling line of individuals. Watch the weather at all times, noting clouds and wind, and if in doubt it is better to return home than strand everyone on an open moor or mountain. Mists form very quickly in such places and it is easy to be lost, even with a map and compass. If you are unable to make it to base due to mist, snow or other severe weather, find a safe place to shelter and await an improvement in conditions. Never wander about aimlessly, since this is the best way to produce accidents. Safety is important at all times – take precautions to avoid dangerous situations.

Camping

Even severely handicapped people enjoy a night under canvas, and camps are a popular out-of-doors activity for schools and groups providing for handicapped young people. Equally the family camping holiday, in caravan or tents, can be considerably enhanced by a greater understanding of one's surroundings and thus provide a suitable environment for development of the handicapped youngster. Often the camp itself will provide enough excitement, but you can also link camps with other activities such as sailing, canoeing or pony trekking. Canoe camps for children from Special Schools are held each summer on the River Tamar, and The Spastics Society has organised activity camps for both sailing and pony trek enthusiasts. Camping may be at a local farm or in a more exotic place – the Isles of Scilly, Brittany or the Swiss Alps. Wherever you want to go, the camp can be exciting and preparations are essentially the same. First you must decide on whether you want to establish an isolated camp, on some hillside farm or in mountain terrain, or visit an organised camp site. While the former may be ideal for mentally handicapped but able-bodied campers, it may be easier for the severe physically handicapped children at a fixed camp site where toilet facilities and showers are provided. This can make life more comfortable for the participants and enable helpers to carry out their tasks under easier conditions. The camp is not so primitive under these circumstances, and cooking may have to be on 'Calor' or 'Gaz' burners rather than the traditional campfire, but the fact of living and sleeping outside is a new experience in itself.

There is a wide range of camping equipment: tents, sleeping bags, tables and chairs, cooking stoves and utensils – if you want advice, visit your local scout headquarters. They will be only too pleased to help you in the planning, and may be prepared to loan some of the gear required. The Scout Association has a branch concerned with the handicapped, and will also give assistance if you contact them. You may wish to prepare new campers in the school grounds by giving them experience of pitching a tent, cooking simple meals out of doors and possibly spending a night under canvas. In this way everyone has more idea of what it's all about before departing on the camp proper. Make a list of the items required and check off everything before you go. Prepare a personal list for each camper, and try to ensure that everyone has a full complement of equipment. Sleeping bags may be a problem for some, but a satisfactory bag can be made from blankets and large blanket pins. Remember, it is essential to be warm at night, and even in summer the night temperature can fall dramatically.

Expeditions

Note: An expedition forms an important part of the Duke of Edinburgh Award Scheme, notably at the Gold Award stage. Other stages of the scheme involve a service project, and an interest and physical activity (or design for living). There is a very wide selection of topics to choose from in each area of the award. An essential feature of the scheme is to show progression over the year, and from one stage to another (bronze, silver, gold). You can discuss a suitable programme for young handicapped people with the Youth Service Officer of the Local Education Authority, and schemes often operate in schools and youth organisations.

While expeditions are certainly not part of the normal life of able-bodied young people, let alone the handicapped, it is true that they form a culmination of scientific observation and recording linked with the rigours of life in an extreme environment. Expeditions can be of a short or long duration, within the British Isles or abroad, but they should stretch the participants both intellectually and physically. A few years ago, in the summer of 1977, I was able to lead a group of young, physically handicapped children from a residential special school, on such an expedition to the High Alps. Planning for the venture began much earlier, and the idea in fact originated three years before our departure. The selection of the location for the expedition was based on finding a place which would present a feeling of isolation, provide environmental rigour but give us reasonable access for wheelchairs and poor walkers. Not least in importance was the need to find an area where we could carry out scientific investigations which might be meaningful over a short period. We decided on the Jungfrau region of the Swiss Alps as providing all that we required; an excellent local rail system into the mountains; a nearby camp site with good facilities, suitable for a base camp; a valley between two adjacent mountain systems, which would be the centre of our environmental studies; and, very important, an exciting atmosphere. We were fortunate that one of our team was able to visit the locality in the year before, and I had previously stayed in the area. It is desirable to obtain as much information as possible beforehand, and we were soon in contact with the Swiss National Tourist Board and the Embassy officials. By the time we departed I had met the six young students who would form half of the group, and we had decided on the project that each would undertake while away. They were shown photographs, maps and travel literature about the region . . . few had been abroad before, and only one had been to Switzerland. Their geography teacher intended to bring Switzerland into the syllabus so that everyone had some idea about our venue. Later, everyone was actually to see what they had previously read about. Planning is just as important as the expedition itself – camping equipment, personal gear, scientific items, food, first aid . . . the list seemed endless but eventually two vehicles, a minibus and a Land Rover, departed with twelve excited travellers and a great deal of luggage!

There followed twelve days of intensive studies in the mountains and valleys, amid dramatic scenery, and often our days stretched from the very early hours of the morning (since we found it cheaper to travel on the mountain railway before 8.00 a.m.) until late at night. We had set up a large work tent, in addition to sleeping tents, where we would cook, eat and carry out laboratory studies in some degree of comfort and organisation. There is no time on an expedition to waste in searching for something you need, and great frustration in wishing you had taken a particular item of equipment!

Gwyn was our geographer – her task was to study the physical aspects of the mountains and valley, the way the land was used, where and how people lived and their transport methods. Her study was so successful that we were able to publish her entire report without any staff assistance. Tony was the expedition botanist, and although he had never looked at a plant before he soon became deeply enthusiastic about his task. He was never without his flower book and a few plants, whether at breakfast or suppertime, and I sometimes thought he ate them by mistake! Both Gwyn and Tony were able to walk and many of their days were spent high up in the mountains, on the Eiger glacier and at 4,300 metres on the Jungfrau. Tony's other claim to fame was his escapade in the deep snow near Eiger, which he saw as a challenge for a walk. He provided a good laugh for everyone when he slipped and slid on his back down a snow slope. Luckily someone had a camera at the ready!

Kathy and Henry were the 'bug-hunters', setting pitfall traps for insects and other small animals from the wooded valley floor up into the mountain tops. We even put traps on a snow field, high on Jungfrau at 4,300 metres, but on our return we were unable to find them again – it had snowed! Some unusual species were encountered, but one old familiar beetle was the seven-spot ladybird, which we found at every site in our collections. While on our way to the Eiger glacier we were lucky to find a colony of alpine newts, living in small ponds created by melting snow. All around was the rich, colourful alpine flora – gentians, globe-flower, snowbells and anemones, all recorded by our cameras. Photography is an excellent way to record plants that you are uncertain about at the time; you can identify them from colour slides on your return.

Our bird-watcher was Andrew – 'Harry' to his friends. All birds observed were compiled into an expedition list of 64 species, many of them new even to the more experienced ornithologists with our party. The middle-spotted woodpecker, citril finch, alpine chough and alpine swift were all species not found in Britain. At high altitude we found the alpine accentor, snow bunting and snowfinch, while lower in the woods of the valley some of us heard the melody of a golden oriole.

The sixth student member of the team was Mark, who was making a survey of small mammals using Longworth live-traps and observing large mammals from their remains. We returned with many bags of bones and droppings! Again all sites were trapped from the valley to mountain scree slopes at 3,000 metres. Shrews, voles and a woodmouse were all recorded, but we found no woodmice in the lower wooded habitats, which surprised us all – until the day we broke camp and found a young individual living amongst our equipment in the tents! The great thrill of opening traps at high altitude to reveal the catch reached a peak when we found snow voles, with thick grey fur coats, on the mountains at Birg. Only very well adapted small mammals could live in such a hostile environment. Some larger mammals were sighted – chamois bounded about the mountain slopes, and as we ascended by cable car we could watch as they scattered among the rocks and crags. Alpine marmot, an exclusively alpine rodent, was sighted from the mountain railway during one journey; and the blue hare and red squirrel were spotted lower in the valley. But without doubt the highlight was the sighting at Eiger of three ibex, the wild goat of Europe. Two males and a female were coming down to browse on the sparse grass, staying in view for five minutes. Once again the cameras were busy.

Finally, upon our return a full account was published in an Expedition Report, which contained in addition to the scientific records and results, a series of personal accounts of the expedition, as seen by each of its student members. As one of them put it!

'I travelled down in the Landrover which made me feel like a young Livingstone about to embark upon the greatest and most dangerous expedition ever attempted.'

BOOK LIST

A Guide to Useful Book Series (* = Paperbacks)

*The Nature Trail Books (Usborne) – excellent for mentally handicapped and young children. Titles include *Trees and Leaves*; *Insect Watching*; *Bird-watching*; *Wild Animals*; *Understanding Farm Animals*; *Ponds and Streams*; *Seashore life*.

*The Spotters' Guides (Usborne) – good illustrations with little text; ideal for the pocket. Have a scorecard which is fun to complete. Suitable for all children. Titles include *Trees*; *Wild flowers*; *Birds*; *Insects*; *Butterflies*; *Fish*; *Seashore*; *Shells*; *Rocks and Minerals*; *Zoo animals*; *Animals*; *Tracks and Signs*; *Ponds and lakes*.

*The Jarold Nature Series Books (Jarrold) – excellent colour photographs and wide subject range. Titles include *Trees*; *Butterflies*; *Birds*; *Rocky shores*; *Sandy shores*; *Seaweeds*; *Fungi*.

*Watch Books (Jarrold) – a new colour series designed for young naturalists. Titles include *Town*; *Garden*; *Landscape*.

The Ladybird Series (Ladybird Books) – some excellent books with plenty of information. Suitable for most abilities of children. Titles include subjects in Natural History; Conservation; History; Geography; Leisure; Out of Door Activities.

*What Happens When (Oliver & Boyd) – well-illustrated studies on local geography; ideal for school studies with slow learners.

*MacDonald Colour Units – Geography (MacDonald) – excellent guides for the teacher; work topics can be modified for slow learners. Titles include weather; maps; transport; town studies; farming; fishing.

Approaches to Environmental Studies (Blandford) – simple treatment of a variety of environmental topics (towns, weather, water, farms); suitable for young able children or older slow-learners.

The Observers Series (Warne) – still a very useful series with some excellent texts and wide subject range; suitable for older brighter children and adults. Useful titles include *Lichens*; *Zoo Animals*; *Ferns*. . . .

The Clue Books (Oxford University Press) – highly recommended for the bright child; good illustrations and keys for identification. Titles include *Insects*; *Trees*; *Freshwater Animals*; *Seashore Animals*; *Flowerless Plants*; *Tracks and Signs*; *Birds*; *Flowers*.

Blandford Colour Series (Blandford) – good colour illustrations for easy identification; able children and adults. Titles include *Pond and Stream Life*; *Mountain Flowers*; *Birds*; *Mushrooms and Toadstools*; *Rocks and Minerals*.

The Young Specialist Books (Burke) – some good identification books for the able child and adult. Titles include *Molluscs*; *Pond Life*; *Seashore*.

Octopus Colour Guides (Octopus Books) – available for a variety of popular animals and plant groups; large colour pictures; some are very good (e.g. *Fish*).

*The Hamlyn All-colour paperbacks (Hamlyn) – good readable texts on natural history; gardening; out of door activities. Older bright children and adults.

Collins Pocket Guide Series (Collins) – the best established series of field guides for the keen naturalist. Titles include *Trees*; *Flowers*; *Seashore*; *Fungi*; *Insects*; *Mammals*; *Birds*; *Reptiles and Amphibia*; *Fish*; *Archaeology*.

The Oxford Book Series (Oxford University Press) – Superb illustrations; suitable for keen naturalists. Titles include *Flowerless Plants*; *Birds*; *Trees*; *Insects*; *Invertebrates*.

The New Naturalist Series (Collins) – without doubt the finest collection of books of wide natural history interest. Over 60 titles.

A new series of booklets and packs designed especially to introduce environmental studies to mentally handicapped and slow-learning children are planned by the Churchtown Farm Field Studies Centre. Entitled *The Churchtown Book of* . . . . they cover a range of topics, the first being on farms. Other titles include flowers and trees; birds; seashore; pond life and city life. The educational packs, called 'Churchtown Nature Project Packs', include a booklet, set of large photographs, student work sheets and teacher/parent project sheets. Based on the work carried out in the past five years at Churchtown Farm Field Studies Centre with many thousands of handicapped young people, they can be obtained by writing directly to the centre.

FURTHER READING

Chapter 1: General

Book of the British Countryside, Drive Publications Ltd, 1973
Botanic Action with David Bellamy, C. Smallman & D. Bellamy, Hutchinson, 1978
Environmental Studies, G. Martin and E. Turner, Blond Educational, 1972
Plant Communities, A. Bülow-Olsen, Penguin, 1978
Schools Projects in Natural History, Devon Trust for Nature Conservation, Heinemann, 1972
The Young Naturalist's Guide to Conservation, N. Arnold, Ward Lock, 1978
The Young Naturalist's Handbook, L. Moore, Hamlyn, 1978

Chapter 2: Towns

A Town Study Companion, G. Bull, Hulton, 1975
Ecology of refuse tips, A. Darlington, Heinemann, 1969
Exploring at Home, P.A. Sauvain, Hulton, 1966
Local geography in Towns, J. Haddon, Philip, 1971
People and Places (no. 2) Towns, T. Crisp, Nelson, 1974
The ecology of towns, A. Leutscher, Franlin Watts, 1975
The roadside wildlife book, R. Mabey, David and Charles, 1974
Wildlife in Britain – a guide to Natural habitats, Safari parks and Zoos, The Automobile Association, 1976

Chapter 3: Parks and Gardens

Book of British Birds, Drive Publications Ltd., 1969
R.S.P.B. Guide to Birdwatching, P. Conder, Hamlyn, 1978
The Hedgerow Book, R. Wilson, David & Charles, 1979
The Tree Key, H. Edlin, Warne, 1978
The natural history of the garden, M. Chinery, Collins, 1977

Chapter 4: Woodlands

Grasses, Ferns, Mosses & Lichens of Great Britain and Ireland, R. Phillips, Pan, 1980
Mammals of Britain. Their tracks, trails & signs, M. Lawrence & R. Brown, Blandford, 1967
Woodland Ecology, E.G. Neal, Heinemann, 1958
Woodlands, W. Condry, Collins, 1974

Chapter 5: Farming and Food

Farming in Britain, F. Hugget, Black, 1975
People and Places 1: Food & Farming, T. Crisp, Nelson, 1974
The Farmer, L.F. Hobley, Allman, 1972
Where does food come from? Althea, Dinosaur Publications, 1976

Chapter 6: Water

Animal Life in Freshwater, H. Mellanby, Methuen, 1963
Fishing, R. Marsden, Macdonald, 1979
Guide to fishing facilities for Disabled Anglers, National Anglers Council, 1977
The Pond Book, J. Dyson, Kestrel, 1976
The world of water, E. Jones, Blandford, 1969
Water sports for the Disabled, The Sports Council, 1978

Chapter 7: Seashore

Beachcombing for beginners, N. Hickin, David & Charles, 1975
British Bivalve Seashells, N. Tebble, British Museum, 1966
Sea Angling, T. Housby, Hodder & Stoughton, 1976
Seawater Aquaria, L.A.J. Jackman, David & Charles, 1974
Shell Life, E. Step, Warne, 1945
The Hamlyn guide to the seashore and shallow seas of Britain and Europe, A.C. Campbell, Hamlyn, 1976
The pebbles on the beach, C. Ellis, Faber, 1954
The Shell Book of Beachcombing, T. Soper, David & Charles, 1972

Chapter 8: Moor and Mountain

Landscape and Atmosphere, J.G. Wilson, Schofield & Sims, 1972
Landscapes of Britain, R. Millward & A. Robinson, David & Charles, 1977

The Backpacker's Handbook, D. Booth, Letts, 1972

The Expedition Handbook, T. Land, Butterworths, 1978

The Extension Activities Handbook, D. Harwood, The Scout Association, 1972

The Usborne Outdoor Book, Usborne, 1979

The World of a Mountain, W. Condry, Faber & Faber, 1977

USEFUL ADDRESSES

Advisory Centre for Education, 32 Trumpington Street, Cambridge.

Calvert Trust, Adventure Centre, Keswick, Cumbria.

Churchtown Farm Field Studies Centre, Lanlivery, Bodmin, Cornwall.

City Farms Advisory Service, Inter-action Trust Ltd, 15, Wilkin Street, London NW5 3NG.

Duke of Edinburgh's Award Office, 5 Prince of Wales Terrace, London W8 5PG.

Forestry Commission, 231 Corstorphine Road, Edinburgh.

National Angler's Council, 5 Cowgate, Peterborough PE1 1PJ.

Harris Biological Supplies, Oldmixon, Weston-Super-Mare (general biology supplier).

Holiday Care Service, 2 Old Bank Chambers, Station Road, Horley, Surrey RH6 9HW.

Peter le Marchant Trust, c/o Colston Bassette House, Colston Bassett, Nottingham NG12 3FE.

Photography for the Disabled, c/o 190 Secrett House, Ham Close, Richmond, Surrey.

Preston Montford Field Centre, Preston Montford Bridge, Shrewsbury.

Riding for the Disabled Association, Avenue R., National Agricultural Centre, Kenilworth, Warks.

R.S.P.B. and Y.O.C., The Lodge, Sandy, Beds.

School Natural Science Society, c/o M.J. Wootton, 44 Claremont Gardens, Upminster, Essex.

Scientific Instruments Ltd, Longworth, Abingdon, Berks. (live traps).

Society for Horticultural therapy and rural training, 51 Catherine Street, Frome, Somerset.

Society for the Promotion of Nature Conservation, The Green, Nettleham, Lincoln. (County conservation trusts).

Thames Cruises, c/o Wansborough Manor, Guildford GU3 2JR.

The Countryside Commission, John Dower House, Crescent Place, Cheltenham, Glos.

The Field Studies Assocation, 62 Wilson Street, London EC2A 2BU.

The Kingfisher Guild, Angling Times, Park House, 117 Park Road, Peterborough PE1 2TS.

The National Trust (Junior Division) Projects Officer, The Old Grape House, Clivedon, Taplow, Maidenhead, Berks.

The Nature Conservancy, (Hedgerow Project) Monks Wood Experimental Station, Abbots Ripon, Huntingdon.

The Scottish Tourist Board, 23 Ravelston Terrace, Edinburgh.

The Scout Association, Baden Powell House, Queen's Gate, London SW7.

The Wildfowl Trust, Slimbridge, Gloucestershire.

Wales Tourist Board, Dept. RG, P.O. Box 151, WDO, Cardiff.

Watch, Advisory Centre for Education, 32 Trumpington Street, Cambridge.

Watkins & Doncaster Ltd, 110 Park View Road, Welling, Kent (entomology equipment).

Wildlife Youth Service, (W.W.F.), Marston Court, 98–106 Manor Road, Wallington, Surrey.

Young Zoologist's Club, London Zoo, Regents Park, London NW1.

Youth Hostels Association, Trevelyan House, St Stephen's Hill, St Albans, Hertfordshire.

INDEX TO PROJECTS AND PRACTICAL WORK

INDEX